Complete Dehydrator Cookbook

Delicious Dehydrator Recipes Including Making Vegetables, Fruits, Meat, Tea & More

Ann Gibbs

Table of Contents

Lettuce

Swiss Chards

Kale Chips

Spinach

Mushrooms

Morel Mushrooms

Cremini Mushrooms

Mushroom Chips

Herbs

Rosemary

Sage

Thyme

Basil

Spices

Ginger Powder

Chili Powder

Onion and Garlic Powder

Nuts

Almonds

Pecans

Pine Nuts

Cashews

Grain and Pasta

Whole Grains

Legumes and Beans

Pasta

Instant Soup Mixes

Onion Soup Mix

Potato Soup Mix

Black Bean Soup Mix

Potato and Chive Soup Mix

Broccoli and Cheddar Soup Mix

Pumpkin and Carrot Soup

Mushroom and Couscous Soup Mix

Flavored tea

Citrus, Berry and Apple Tea

Apple, Strawberries, Hibiscus and Rose Tea

Meat

Ground Turkey Jerky

Teriyaki Beef Jerky

Chicken

Lamb Jerky

Ground Beef

Teriyaki Mushroom Jerky

Fish

Salmon Jerky

Tuna

Shrimps

Crab

Dairy

Milk Powder

Butter Powder

Eggs

Cheese

Yogurt

Breakfasts

Pumpkin and Chia Oats

Buckwheat Granola

Brown Rice Cereal

Chia Seeds Porridge

Buckwheat Porridge

Snacks

Sweet Potato Chips

Potato Chips

Corn Chips

Parmesan Tomato Chips

Fruit Roll-Ups

Vegetarian Dishes

Mixed Vegetables and Beans Soup

Vegetable and Bean Soup with Garlic and Tomato

Eggplant Jerky

Buffalo Cauliflower Popcorn

Vegan Dishes

Red Lentil Chili

Vegetable Yellow Curry

Sriracha Chickpeas

Chickpea and Spinach Curry

Lentil Stew

Backpacking and Camper Foods

Mushroom Risotto

Beef Alfredo

Chickpea and Vegetable Curry

Cheesy Salmon Pasta

Mac and Cheese

Just-Add-Water Recipes

Ground Beef and Beans Chili

Taco Stew

Jarred Garden Vegetable Soup

Bread and Crackers

Flax Seed Bread

Bread Crumbs

Peanut Butter and Banana Graham Crackers

Bagel Flax Crackers

Desserts

Caramel Apple Chips

Apple and Flax Seeds Cookies

Raisin Cookies

Marshmallows

Peanut Butter Balls

Beverages

Introduction

Are you looking for a way to store your food more effectively? Do you want to create an inventory of ingredients that will help you in emergencies? Are you on a diet and want to eat more healthily? Then, a food dehydrator should be the first thing you set at your kitchen counter. A Food Dehydrator is a kitchen appliance, equal to the size of a toaster that is used to dry or dehydrate different types of foods like meat and vegetables. To "dehydrate" means to draw out moisture and all water content from the food that is being placed in it. This makes the food last longer than they would if they had their moisture, but it doesn't affect other nutrients in any way. You can put a sliced up apple inside the device, and it will still have all of its iron, sugar, fiber, and vitamins. This is the reason why many health-conscious people prefer dehydrated foods rather than cooked meals. In cooking, the fresh ingredients lose their nutrition.

There are numerous ways of preparing food nowadays, all bringing a unique flavor profile to the table. Dehydrating food is also one such way with additional benefits attached to it. The prepared food can be used for up to 2 to 3 years. If you have a surplus of any ingredients, a smart way to preserve them would be dehydrating. You don't need any chemical baths or freezers. Also, because the prepared food doesn't get spoiled, it can be used in an emergency pantry or for long journeys and hikes. People can also just eat them as healthy and delicious snacks. There are endless benefits achieved by using only this small device, and this book will show you how to take full use of it.

Why to Dehydrate Food?

There are plenty of benefits of using a dehydrator and some advantages that you may never heard of. It's time for you to realize the potential of this versatile machine so you can reap all the goodness as well.

- It makes your ingredients more delicious

  By dehydrating your food, you are removing water and increasing the concentration of its nutrients. It makes the ingredient more flavorful within every bite. A richer flavor profile will produce a tastier meal. It is also much better tasting than store-bought dehydrated foods because they might have been sitting on the shelves for a very long time, and you should know the freshness of your ingredients.

- It helps you in savings

  Buying snacks from stores with vegetables and fruits can be pricey, and if you want to have organic alternatives plus freshness, they can go right out of your budget. Dehydrating food can serve as a snack making machine removing the need of ever buying snacks again. Also, you can get vegetables and fruits in their peak season when they are plentiful and inexpensive. Then you can dehydrate them for future use. All these methods will help you save up with no compromise on health.

- It helps you to be healthy

  When you are dehydrating your foods, there is no use of any additives or preservatives, which the store-bought ones will contain. You are eating only that fresh vegetables, fruits, or whatever food that you are using with its nutrients intact. Moreover, it is a healthy switch from salty chips and sweet candies. They will help you with your snack cravings when you are on a strict dieting plan.

- You can carry them anywhere

  Fruits and other healthy ingredients are heavy, occupy a lot of space, and usually make a lot of mess. When you dehydrate the same fruits or any ingredient, they become more compact and light. You can store them in a can or a bag and munch on them anywhere. You can place it in a children's lunchbox, a car, or beside your electronics while you work.

- It helps us reduce wastes

  If you start using your dehydrator, you will never have to throw away food again. There are two ways you can reduce wasting. Firstly, if you have a small garden and you have a surplus amount of vegetables and fruits, you can dry them and store them. Secondly, if you have food spoiling, you can dry them and make them last for much longer. Moreover, there is a great problem of food wasting all over the world, and dehydrating can decrease our habits of throwing away food.

- You can store effectively

  After you dehydrate food, they shrink in size and occupy a fraction of its original volume. You can fill more of your food. They don't need a freezer or any type of special environment. You can place them in jars or plastic bags and place them on a shelf for years to come.

- You can have effective dehydration

  A dehydrator makes dehydrating look very simple. If you want to use any other devices, they will not be as effective. Using an oven will drive up costs and slightly cook the foods that you want to preserve. A dehydrator doesn't use high temperatures as an oven, and so it isn't as expensive to use. It will take all the moisture out and still leave your ingredients raw. Raw food has much more nutrition than cooked ones, so using a dehydrator would be your first choice.

- You can do many things with it

  There are many ways to use this incredible tool and for many purposes. You can jerky out of leftover meat, dry up fruits to make them taste sweeter before adding to a dish, make healthy snacks by dehydrating vegetables, and making them into chips. You can even use it to make pet treats that have no additives and preservatives. There are many things to do with cheeses and bread that accompany your breakfast. If you are proactive enough, you can make even better use of this device then mentioned here.

How Does Dehydration Work?

A dehydrator uses heat to pull out the water from the foods that you want to dehydrate. It is an electrical kitchen appliance that has four parts: fan, heating element, vent, and layers of trays.

The heating element is the most important because it raises the temperature of the device for dehydration to take place. It exposes the food to a moderately raised temperature for a long period. This process effectively takes all the moisture out, but leaves the nutrients and the flavors of the food undisturbed. The high temperature would cook rather than dehydrate its contents. There is a fan attached to the device, which distributes that heat by circulating the air around the device. The device dehydrates all the tray compartments equally because of this fan.

It is not just about raising the temperature to lose water; you need to prevent it from getting back in the food as well. The fan circulates the air in and out of the vents constantly, exposing the food to dry air and throwing away the moisture out of the device.

How to Dehydrate Food?

The dehydrator has a set of temperatures to choose from, which is necessary because different foods need to be set at different temperatures. Also, the time required depends upon the type of food that you want to dehydrate. Many types of dehydrators are available in the market, so you need to have a clear mind of what you want to do with this device and purchase the perfect one.

If you want to dehydrate huge portions of food, purchasing a big dehydrator would be a smart choice. Square dehydrators are better than round ones because they give more surface area to work with. Invest in a dehydrator with a lot of temperature settings and a timer for better control.

Almost all foods can be dehydrated except for high fatty foods and dairy products. Meat and vegetables need to be blanched or cooked before putting in the machine, but fruits generally don't require it. Entire meals like soups and sauces can be dehydrated as well, but they would need parchment paper or the device's paper.

Two methods can dehydrate fruits. They can be sliced and placed on a tray in the form of chips. They can also be blended and spread on parchment paper and rehydrated as pudding.

Vegetables need to be blanched if you want to rehydrate them and cook them later on. Otherwise, there is no need. It's better to use frozen vegetables but avoid canned vegetables because they're too wet.

Meat can be dried as well, but it's better to use lean meat and not the ones with high-fat content.

How to Store Dehydrated Food?

If you dehydrate your foods properly, they can last a long time and become your great friend at times of emergency. If you are sure that the food you will dry will be consumed within a year, then you should place them in a freezer bag or a storage bag. Squeeze out excess air as much as possible. If you are not sure and want them to last longer, vacuum seal them and keep them in a cold, dark place. Meats and seafood don't last as long as fruits and vegetables. If you are sure you will consume your dried meat and seafood within a month, then store them in storage bags and place them in a cold dark place. If you are not sure and want them to last longer, then vacuum-seal them.

How to Avoid Common Mistakes During Dehydration of Foods?

When using a new device, it is expected that there would be some mistakes. Here is a list of common mistakes to avoid when using this appliance.

- Don't stack the ingredients over each other

Many people make this mistake, which should be entirely avoided. The stacking of sliced foods will result in partial dehydration and wastage of time and energy. Space your food out evenly on trays so that they don't touch each other.

- Properly blanching vegetables

Blanching is a process of boiling a certain ingredient for a few minutes and then putting them into cold water. If you do it improperly, then your vegetables will not rehydrate properly, and then you can't use them to be cooked.

- Cut your foods evenly

Most beginners will have a difficult time uniformly cutting their food, but this is very important. This will ensure that every slice of that food dehydrates at the same time. If not, you will have to regularly check whether the process is done or not, and some of your dried food can be over dried.

- Use the device in properly ventilated places

When you are using the machine, it will produce a lot of moisture and may produce a lot of smell as well. This is especially a problem if you are dehydrating peppers or onions. This can irritate the people around the house as well if you don't place it properly.

Strawberries

Preparation time: 10 minutes

Dehydration time: 14 hours

Ingredients:

- Whole strawberries, fresh

Instructions:

- Clean the strawberries by rinsing them under cold running water into a colander so that there is no dirt on them.
- Remove the leaves, cut out the stem, release the core by using a sharp knife, and then cut the berries into even slices, about ¼-inch thick.

- Switch on the dehydrator, then set it to 135 degrees F, and when it preheats, arrange strawberry slices in a single layer on the dehydrator trays with ½-inch space between the slices.

- Shut the dehydrator with its lid and then let the berries dry for 8 to 10 hours or 10 to 14 hours until crisp.

- When done, turn off the dehydrator, open the lid and let the berries cool for 30 minutes at room temperature.

- Check the dryness of berries by breaking its slice in half, and there shouldn't be any moisture along the surface of the break.

- Transfer the berries into airtight containers, fill the containers about two-third, cover with the lids and store them in a cool and dry place, away from heat or direct light.

Blueberries

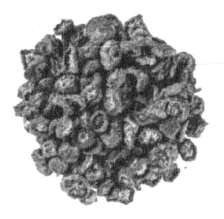

Preparation time: 10 minutes

Dehydration time: 30 hours

Ingredients:

- Blueberries, fresh

Instructions:

- Rinse the blueberries under cold running water into a colander until clean, pat dry with the paper towels, and then make a small hole in each berry by poking it.
- Switch on the dehydrator, then set it to 135 degrees F, and when it preheats, arrange berries in a single layer on the dehydrator trays with ½-inch space between them.
- Shut with its lid, and then let the berries dry for 24 to 30 hours until completely dry and shrink.
- When done, turn off the dehydrator, open the lid and let the berries cool for 30 minutes at room temperature.
- Check the dryness of berries by breaking a berry, and there shouldn't be any moisture along the surface of the break.
- Transfer the berries into airtight containers, fill the containers about two-third, cover with the lids and store them in a cool and dry place, away from heat or direct light.

Cherries

Preparation time: 10 minutes

Dehydration time: 23 hours

Ingredients:

- Cherries, fresh

Instructions:

- Rinse the cherries under cold running water into a colander until cleaned and then pat dry with the paper towels.
- Remove the stems and then pit the cherries by using a cherry pitter.
- Switch on the dehydrator, then set it to 165 degrees F or the highest temperature, and when it preheats, arrange the cherries in a single layer on the dehydrator trays with ½-inch space between them.
- Shut the dehydrator with its lid, let the berries dry for 3 hours, then switch the temperature of the dehydrator to 135 degrees F and continue drying for 10 to 20 hours until

completely dry but still pliable; drying time depends on the size of cherries.

- When done, turn off the dehydrator, open the lid and let the berries cool for 30 minutes at room temperature.
- Check the dryness of cherries by breaking a cherry, and there shouldn't be any moisture along the surface of the break.
- Transfer the cherries into airtight containers, fill the containers about two-third, cover with the lids and store them in a cool and dry place, away from heat or direct light.

Peaches

Preparation time: 10 minutes

Dehydration time: 36 hours and 30 minutes

Ingredients:

- Whole peaches, fresh

Instructions:

- Prepare the peaches, and for this, use a paring knife to make a small X in its bottom.
- Take a large pot half full with water, place it over high heat, bring the water to boil, then add peaches and boil them for 1 minute.
- Then transfer peaches to a large bowl by using a slotted spoon, let them rest until cool enough to handle and peel the skin from peaches.
- Take a large bowl, pour in 4 cups water, stir in 1 ½ tablespoon of vinegar and then drop in peeled peaches.
- Working on one peach at a time, remove and discard its pit, then cut the flesh into ¼-inch thick slices and return the slices into the vinegar-water mixture.
- When done, drain the peach slices into a colander and then set aside until required.
- Switch on the dehydrator, then set it to 135 degrees F, and when it preheats, arrange the slices in a single layer on the dehydrator trays with ½-inch space between them.
- Shut the dehydrator with its lid, and then let the peach dry for 20 to 36 hours until completely dry but still pliable.
- When done, turn off the dehydrator, open the lid and let the peach slices cool for 30 minutes at room temperature.
- Check the dryness of peaches by breaking its slice, and there shouldn't be any moisture along the surface of the break.
- Transfer the peach slices into airtight containers, fill the containers about two-third, cover with the lids and store them in a cool and dry place, away from heat or direct light.

Citrus Slices

Preparation time: 10 minutes

Dehydration time: 12 hours

Ingredients:

- Any citrus fruit like oranges, grapefruit, kumquats, limes, lemons

Instructions:

- Scrub and rinse the fruits under cold running water until clean, pat dry with the paper towels, and then slice the fruits crosswire into discs, about ¼-inch thick.
- Switch on the dehydrator, then set it to 135 degrees F or the medium-high temperature, and when it preheats, arrange the slices in a single layer on the dehydrator trays with ½-inch space between them

- Shut the dehydrator with its lid, let the slices dry for 12 hours or more until completely dry but still pliable; drying time depends on the thickness of slices.
- When done, turn off the dehydrator, open the lid and let the berries cool for 30 minutes at room temperature.
- Check the dryness of slice; the flesh should not be moist but tacky, and the pith may be slightly curled and spongy.
- Transfer the slices into airtight containers, fill the containers about two-third, cover with the lids and store in a cool and dry place, away from heat or direct light.

Cabbage

Preparation time: 10 minutes

Dehydration time: 11 hours

Ingredients:

- Cabbage, green, white, red, napa or bok choy

Instructions:

- Remove the outer leaves of cabbage, remove the stem or core, rinse thoroughly under running water and then pat dry with paper towels.

- Then cut the cabbage into quarters and cut each quarter into the 1/8-inch thick strip.
- Switch on the dehydrator, then set it to 135 degrees F, and when it preheats, arrange the cabbage slices in a single layer on the dehydrator trays with ½-inch space between them.
- Shut the dehydrator with its lid, and then let the zucchini slices dry for 8 to 11 hours until completely dry and crisp but still pliable.
- When done, turn off the dehydrator, open the lid and let the peach slices cool for 30 minutes at room temperature.
- Check the dryness of cabbage by breaking its slice, and there shouldn't be any moisture along the surface of the break.
- Transfer the cabbage into airtight containers, fill the containers about two-third, cover with the lids and store them in a cool and dry place, away from heat or direct light.

Zucchini

Preparation time: 10 minutes

Dehydration time: 6 hours and 30 minutes

Ingredients:

- Zucchini or summer squash

Instructions:

- Scrub and rinse the zucchini under cold running water until clean, pat dry with the paper towels, and then slice into rounds, about ¼-inch thick.
- Take a large pot half full with water, place it over high heat, bring the water to boil, then add zucchini slices and boil them for 1 minute.
- Then transfer zucchini to a large bowl containing ice-cold water and let them rest for 15 minutes until cooled.
- Switch on the dehydrator, then set it to 135 degrees F, and when it preheats, arrange the zucchini slices in a single layer on the dehydrator trays with ½-inch space between them.

- Shut the dehydrator with its lid, and then let the zucchini slices dry for 6 hours until completely dry and crisp but still pliable.
- When done, turn off the dehydrator, open the lid and let the peach slices cool for 10 minutes at room temperature.
- Check the dryness of peaches by breaking its slice, and there shouldn't be any moisture along the surface of the break.
- Transfer the zucchini slices into airtight containers, fill the containers about two-third, cover with the lids and store them in a cool and dry place, away from heat or direct light.

Tomato

Preparation time: 10 minutes

Dehydration time: 6 hours

Ingredients:

- Roma tomatoes

Instructions:

- Rinse the tomato under cold running water until clean, and then pat dry with the paper towels.
- Slice the tomatoes lengthwise, about ¼-inch thick and then use a tip of a peeler to remove the seed gel, don't puncture the skin.
- Switch on the dehydrator, then set it to 135 degrees F, and when it preheats, arrange the tomato slices in a single layer skin-side-down on the dehydrator trays with ½-inch space between the slices.
- Shut the dehydrator with its lid, and then let the tomato dry for 6 to 8 hours until it starts to crisp.
- When done, turn off the dehydrator, open the lid and let the tomatoes cool for 15 minutes at room temperature.
- Check the dryness of tomatoes by breaking its slice in half, and there shouldn't be any moisture along the surface of the break.
- Transfer the tomato slices into an airtight plastic bag, store in a cool and dry place, away from heat or direct light, or freeze for up to 6 to 9 months.
- When ready to use, place tomatoes in a heatproof dish, cover with water, and then microwave for 2 minutes at a high heat setting.

Onion Flakes

Preparation time: 10 minutes

Dehydration time: 12 hours

Ingredients:

- White onions, fresh

Instructions:

- Prepare the onions, and for this, cut off the two ends, peel their skin, then cut each onion in half and cut into slices, about ¼-inch thick.
- Switch on the dehydrator, then set it to 125 degrees F, and when it preheats, arrange onion slices in a single layer on the dehydrator trays with ½-inch space between the slices.
- Shut the dehydrator with its lid and then let the berries dry for 12 hours until completely dry and leathery.
- When done, turn off the dehydrator, open the lid and let the berries cool for 15 minutes at room temperature.

- Check the dryness of onion by breaking its slice in half, and there shouldn't be any moisture along the surface of the break.
- Crumble the dehydrated onion in a blender or transfer the onion into airtight containers, fill the containers about two-third, cover with the lids and store in a cool and dry place, away from heat or direct light.

Potato Flakes

Preparation time: 10 minutes

Dehydration time: 6 hours and 20 minutes

Ingredients:

- 5 large potatoes

Instructions:

- Prepare the potatoes, and for this, peel them and chop them into bite-size pieces.

- Transfer the potatoes into a large pot, cover them with water, then place the pot over medium heat and bring to boil.

- Continue boiling the potatoes for 10 to 15 minutes or until soft enough to mash and then drain potatoes into a colander.

- Transfer potatoes into a large bowl and then mash by using a fork until smooth.

- Switch on the dehydrator, then set it to 145 degrees F, line the dehydrator trays with parchment sheet, and when it preheats, spread mashed potatoes in a thin layer.

- Shut the dehydrator with its lid, and then let the berries dry for 6 hours until completely dry.

- When done, turn off the dehydrator, open the lid and let the potato cool for 15 minutes at room temperature.

- Then break the potato into chunks, transfer into a blender and then pulse for 1 to 2 minutes at high speed until the mixture resembles flakes.

- Transfer the potato flakes into airtight containers, fill the containers about two-third, cover with the lids and store them in a cool and dry place, away from heat or direct light.

- When ready to use, bring water to boil in a pot, stir in potato flask, then remove the pot from heat, add more ingredients to adjust taste and then serve.

Scallions

Preparation time: 5 minutes

Dehydration time: 6 hours

Ingredients:

- Scallions

Instructions:

- Prepare the scallions, and for this, cut off their root ends and damaged ends and then rinse well under running water until clean.
- Chop the scallions into uniform pieces and then separate white and green parts.
- Switch on the dehydrator, then set it to 95 degrees F, and when it preheats, arrange white and green parts separately in a single layer on the dehydrator trays.
- Shut the dehydrator with its lid and then let the berries dry for 4 to 5 hours until completely dry.
- When done, turn off the dehydrator, open the lid and let the onions cool for 15 minutes at room temperature.
- Powder the dehydrated onion in a blender or transfer onions straight away into airtight containers, fill the

containers about two-third, cover with the lids and store them in a cool and dry place, away from heat or direct light.

Frozen Vegetables

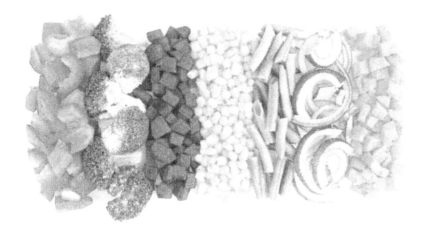

Preparation time: 5 minutes

Dehydration time: 6 hours

Ingredients:

- 1 pack of frozen vegetables like peas, carrots, mixed veggies

Instructions:

- Break the chunks of vegetables, and if there is ice, let the vegetables sit for 1 hour at room temperature until some of the ice melts and then soak excess moisture by paper towels.
- Switch on the dehydrator, then set it to 125 degrees F, and when it preheats, arrange vegetables separately in a single layer on the dehydrator trays.

- Shut the dehydrator with its lid and then let the berries dry for 6 hours until completely dry; keep eyes on the vegetables as some may be dried quickly than others like bulky veggies.
- When done, turn off the dehydrator, open the lid and let the berries cool for 15 minutes at room temperature.
- Power the dehydrated vegetables in a blender to use as a vegetable powder or transfer directly into a plastic bag or airtight containers, fill the containers about two-third, cover with the lids and store in a cool and dry place, away from heat or direct light.

Corn

Preparation time: 10 minutes

Dehydration time: 12 hours and 15 minutes

Ingredients:

- A batch of sweet corn cobs

Instructions:

- Blanch the corn, and for this, husk them, place corn cobs in a large pot and cover with water.
- Place the pot over high heat, bring the water to boil, and then let corn boil for 4 minutes.
- After 4 minutes, transfer corn to a large bowl containing ice-chilled water, let them sit for 10 minutes, and then drain into a colander.
- Cut a slice from the bottom of cob, hold the cob vertically and then run a knife down its side to cut corn kernels from the cob.
- Switch on the dehydrator, then set it to 125 degrees F, and when it preheats, spread corn kernels in a single layer on the dehydrator trays.
- Shut the dehydrator with its lid, and then let the berries dry for 8 to 12 hours until completely dry but still brittle.
- When done, turn off the dehydrator, open the lid and let the corn cool for 1 hour at room temperature.
- Transfer the corn into airtight containers, fill the containers about two-third, cover with the lids and store them in a cool and dry place, away from heat or direct light.

Lettuce

Preparation time: 10 minutes

Dehydration time: 8 hours

Ingredients:

- Bunch of lettuce

Instructions:

- Remove lettuce leaves from its head, cut off any damaged parts and fibrous membrane at the bottom of each leaf, and then let the leaves soak in ice-cold water for 15 minutes.

- Drain the lettuce leaves, rinse well under running water until clean, and then pat dry with a kitchen towel or use a salad spinner.
- Switch on the dehydrator, then set it to 105 degrees F, and when it preheats, arrange lettuce leaves in a single layer on the dehydrator trays with ½-inch space between the slices.
- Shut the dehydrator with its lid and then let the berries dry for 4 to 8 hours until completely dry.
- When done, turn off the dehydrator, open the lid and let the lettuce cool for 15 minutes at room temperature.
- Check the dryness of lettuce by breaking its leaf, and there shouldn't be any moisture along the surface of the break.
- Transfer the lettuce into airtight containers, fill the containers about two-third, cover with the lids and store them in a cool and dry place, away from heat or direct light.

Swiss Chards

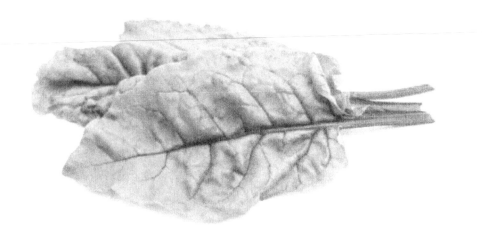

Preparation time: 5 minutes

Dehydration time: 8 hours

Ingredients:

- Swiss chards

Instructions:

- Rinse the chards under running water until clean, remove any damaged parts, pat dry with a kitchen towel or use a salad spinner, and then cut into ¼-inch pieces.
- Switch on the dehydrator, then set it to 135 degrees F, and when it preheats, arrange Swiss chards in a single layer on the dehydrator trays with ½-inch space between the slices.
- Shut the dehydrator with its lid and then let the berries dry for 4 to 8 hours until completely dry.
- When done, turn off the dehydrator, open the lid and let the lettuce cool for 15 minutes at room temperature.
- Check the dryness of chards by breaking its leaf, and there shouldn't be any moisture along the surface of the break.
- Transfer the chards into airtight containers, fill the containers about two-third, cover with the lids and store them in a cool and dry place, away from heat or direct light.

Kale Chips

Preparation time: 10 minutes

Dehydration time: 5 hours

Ingredients:

- 1 large bunch of kale
- ¾ teaspoon salt
- ¼ teaspoon cayenne pepper
- 2 tablespoons nutritional yeast
- 3 teaspoons olive oil

Instructions:

- Remove kale leaves from its stalks, rinse the kale under running water until clean, and then pat dry with a kitchen towel or use a salad spinner.
- Place the kale leaves into a large bowl, add salt and oil and then massage the leaves for 1 minute until all the leaves are evenly coated with salt and oil.
- Add cayenne pepper and yeast and then toss until well coated.

- Switch on the dehydrator, then set it to 145 degrees F, and when it preheats, arrange kale leaves in a single layer on the dehydrator trays with ½-inch space between the slices.
- Shut the dehydrator with its lid, let kale dry for 1 hour, then switch the temperature to 115 degrees F and continue drying for 4 hours until completely dry and crisp.
- When done, turn off the dehydrator, open the lid and let the kale cool for 15 minutes at room temperature.
- Check the dryness of kale by breaking its leaf, and there shouldn't be any moisture along the surface of the break.
- Transfer the kale into airtight containers, fill the containers about two-third, cover with the lids and store them in a cool and dry place, away from heat or direct light.

Spinach

Preparation time: 5 minutes

Dehydration time: 6 hours

Ingredients:

- Bunches of spinach leaves, fresh

Instructions:

- Rinse the spinach under running water until clean, and then pat dry with a kitchen towel or use a salad spinner.
- Switch on the dehydrator, then set it to 125 degrees F, and when it preheats, arrange spinach in a single layer on the dehydrator trays with ½-inch space between the slices.
- Shut the dehydrator with its lid and then let the berries dry for 4 to 6 hours until completely dry.
- When done, turn off the dehydrator, open the lid and let the spinach cool for 15 minutes at room temperature.
- Check the dryness of spinach by breaking its leaf, and there shouldn't be any moisture along the surface of the break.
- Power the dried spinach or transfer directly into airtight containers, fill the containers about two-third, cover with the lids and store in a cool and dry place, away from heat or direct light.

Morel Mushrooms

Preparation time: 15 minutes

Dehydration time: 8 hours

Ingredients:

- 2 pounds morel mushrooms
- 2 tablespoons salt
- 8 cups of water

Instructions:

- Scrub and rinse the mushrooms until clean, pat dry with paper towels and then cut each in half lengthwise.

- Take a large bowl, pour in water, stir in salt, then add mushrooms and let them soak for a minimum of 10 minutes or 30 minutes.
- Then drain the mushrooms, rinse thoroughly, gently squeeze them and then pat dry with paper towels.
- Switch on the dehydrator, then set it to 125 degrees F, and when it preheats, arrange mushrooms in a single layer on the dehydrator trays with ½-inch space between the slices.
- Shut the dehydrator with its lid and then let the mushrooms dry for 4 to 8 hours until completely dry, dehydrating time depends on the size of the mushrooms.
- When done, turn off the dehydrator, open the lid and let the mushrooms cool for 15 minutes at room temperature.
- Check the dryness of mushrooms by breaking its slice in half, and there shouldn't be any moisture along the surface of the break.
- Powder the dehydrated mushrooms in a blender or transfer them directly into airtight containers, fill the containers about two-third, cover with the lids and store in a cool and dry place, away from heat or direct light.

Cremini Mushrooms

Preparation time: 10 minutes

Dehydration time: 12 hours

Ingredients:

- Cremini mushrooms, fresh

Instructions:

- Scrub and rinse the mushrooms until clean, pat dry with paper towels and then cut into slices, about ¼-inch thick.
- Take a large bowl, pour in water, stir in salt, then add mushrooms and let them soak for a minimum of 10 minutes or 30 minutes.
- Switch on the dehydrator, then set it to 100 degrees F, and when it preheats, arrange mushrooms in a single layer on the dehydrator trays with ½-inch space between the slices.
- Shut the dehydrator with its lid and then let the mushrooms dry for 8 to 12 hours until completely dry, dehydrating time depends on the thickness of the mushrooms slices.

- When done, turn off the dehydrator, open the lid and let the mushrooms cool for 15 minutes at room temperature.
- Check the dryness of mushrooms by breaking its slice in half, and there shouldn't be any moisture along the surface of the break.
- Powder the dehydrated mushrooms in a blender or transfer them directly into airtight containers, fill the containers about two-third, cover with the lids and store in a cool and dry place, away from heat or direct light.

Mushroom Chips

Preparation time: 10 minutes

Dehydration time: 6 hours

Ingredients:

- 4 cups mushrooms with caps

- ½ teaspoon garlic powder
- ½ teaspoon of sea salt
- ½ teaspoon dried parsley
- 1 tablespoon lemon juice

Instructions:

- Prepare the mushrooms, and for this, trim their ends and then cut into slices, about 1/8-inch thick.
- Take a large bowl, place the mushroom slices in it, add remaining ingredients and then toss until evenly coated.
- Switch on the dehydrator, then set it to 135 degrees F, and when it preheats, arrange mushroom slices in a single layer on the dehydrator trays with ½-inch space between the slices.
- Shut the dehydrator with its lid, and then let the mushroom dry for 4 to 6 hours until completely dry and crisp.
- When done, turn off the dehydrator, open the lid and let the mushrooms cool for 15 minutes at room temperature.
- Serve straight away or transfer the mushrooms chips into airtight containers or a plastic bag, fill it about two-third, and then store in a cool and dry place, away from heat or direct light.

Rosemary

Preparation time: 10 minutes

Dehydration time: 8 hours

Ingredients:

- Bunch of rosemary, fresh

Instructions:

- Rinse the rosemary under running water until sprigs have cleaned, shake off excess moisture, and then spread them on a tray lined with paper towels for 45 minutes or more until dry.

- Switch on the dehydrator, then set it to 95 degrees F, and when it preheats, arrange rosemary sprigs in a single layer on the dehydrator trays with ½-inch space between the slices.

- Shut the dehydrator with its lid and then let the berries dry for 6 to 8 hours until completely dry and crisp.
- When done, turn off the dehydrator, open the lid and let the berries cool for 10 minutes at room temperature.
- After 10 minutes, gather all the sprigs, twist them back and forth to separate leaves from stems, and then pick out little stems.
- Powder the dehydrated rosemary leaves in a blender or transfer them directly into airtight containers, fill the containers about two-third, cover with the lids and store in a cool and dry place, away from heat or direct light.

Sage

Preparation time: 5 minutes

Dehydration time: 4 hours

Ingredients:

- Bunch of sage, fresh

Instructions:

- Separate sage leaves from its stems, rinse thoroughly under running water and then pat dry with paper towels.
- Switch on the dehydrator, then set it to 125 degrees F, and when it preheats, arrange sage leaves in a single layer on the dehydrator trays.
- Shut the dehydrator with its lid and then let the sage dry for 1 to 4 hours until completely dry and crisp.
- When done, turn off the dehydrator, open the lid and let the sage cool for 10 minutes at room temperature.
- Check the dryness of sage by breaking its leaf, and it should crumble.
- Powder the dehydrated sage leaves in a blender or transfer them directly into airtight containers, fill the containers about two-third, cover with the lids and store in a cool and dry place, away from heat or direct light.

Thyme

Preparation time: 5 minutes

Dehydration time: 6 hours

Ingredients:

- Bunches of thyme

Instructions:

- Prepare the thyme, and for this, cut off their ends, remove and discard bad sprigs.
- Then rinse thyme thoroughly until running water until cleaned and remove excess water by using a salad spinner or let them rest on paper towels for 30 minutes or more until dry.
- Switch on the dehydrator, then set it to 115 degrees F, and when it preheats, arrange thyme sprigs in a single layer.
- Shut the dehydrator with its lid, and then let the thyme dry for 4 to 6 hours until completely dry and crisp.
- When done, turn off the dehydrator, open the lid and let the berries cool for 10 minutes at room temperature.

- Gather all the sprigs, twist them back and forth to separate leaves from stems.
- Powder the dehydrated thyme leaves in a blender or transfer them directly into airtight containers, fill the containers about two-third, cover with the lids and store in a cool and dry place, away from heat or direct light.

Basil

Preparation time: 5 minutes

Dehydration time: 24 hours

Ingredients:

- Basil leaves, fresh

Instructions:

- Cut off the stems from basil leaves, rinse the leaves under running water until clean, and then remove excess water by using a salad spinner or let them rest on paper towels for 30 minutes or more until dry.

- Switch on the dehydrator, then set it to 115 degrees F, and when it preheats, arrange basil leaves in a single layer on the dehydrator trays with ½-inch space between the slices.

- Shut the dehydrator with its lid, and then let the basil dry for 12 to 24 hours until completely dry and crisp.

- When done, turn off the dehydrator, open the lid and let the basil cool for 10 minutes at room temperature.

- Crumble the dehydrated rosemary leaves or transfer them directly into airtight containers, fill the containers about two-third, cover with the lids and store in a cool and dry place, away from heat or direct light.

Ginger Powder

Preparation time: 10 minutes

Dehydration time: 2 hours

Ingredients:

- Ginger root

Instructions:

- Prepare the ginger, and for this, scrub it and rinse well under running water.
- Then peel the ginger and cut it into slices, about ¼-inch thick.

- Switch on the dehydrator, then set it to 150 degrees F, and when it preheats, arrange ginger slices in a single layer on the dehydrator trays with ½-inch space between the slices.
- Shut the dehydrator with its lid and then let the ginger dry for 1 hour and 30 minutes to 2 hours until completely dry and pliable.
- When done, turn off the dehydrator, open the lid and let the ginger cool for 30 minutes at room temperature.
- Check the dryness of ginger by breaking its slice in half, and there shouldn't be any moisture along the surface of the break.
- Powder the dehydrated ginger in a blender, strain out the ginger powder to remove any large chunks in it, and then transfer it into an airtight container.
- Cover the containers with the lids and then store them in a cool and dry place, away from heat or direct light.

Chili Powder

Preparation time: 10 minutes

Dehydration time: 8 hours

Ingredients:

- Red chili peppers

Instructions:

- Prepare the peppers, and for this, rinse well under running water, and cut off the stems and any rotting parts.
- Pat dry the peppers with paper towels and then cut them into rings.
- Switch on the dehydrator, then set it to 140 degrees F, and when it preheats, arrange pepper rings in a single layer on the dehydrator trays with ½-inch space between the slices.
- Shut the dehydrator with its lid and then let the pepper rings dry for 5 hours to 8 hours until completely dry and pliable, the dehydrating time depends on the thickness of the pepper walls.
- When done, turn off the dehydrator, open the lid and let the berries cool for 15 minutes at room temperature.
- Powder the dehydrated pepper rings in a blender, strain out the chili powder to remove any large chunks in it, and then transfer it into an airtight container.
- Cover the containers with the lids and then store them in a cool and dry place, away from heat or direct light.

Onion and Garlic Powder

Preparation time: 10 minutes

Dehydration time: 12 hours

Ingredients:

- White onions, peeled
- Garlic cloves, peeled

Instructions:

- Rinse the peeled onions and garlic and then chop them.
- Then peel the ginger and cut it into slices, about ¼-inch thick.
- Switch on the dehydrator, then set it to 125 degrees F, and when it preheats, arrange chopped onion and garlic in a single layer on the dehydrator trays with ½-inch space between the slices.
- Shut the dehydrator with its lid and then let the onion and garlic dry for 6 to 12 hours until completely dry and crispy.

- When done, turn off the dehydrator, open the lid and let the onion and garlic cool for 30 minutes at room temperature.
- Powder the dehydrated onion and garlic in a blender, strain out the onion and garlic powder to remove any large chunks in it, and then transfer it into an airtight container.
- Cover the containers with the lids and then store them in a cool and dry place, away from heat or direct light.

Almonds

Preparation time: 10 minutes

Dehydration time: 24 hours

Ingredients:

- 4 cups almonds
- 1 tablespoon of sea salt
- Water as needed

Instructions:

- Take a large bowl, add almonds, pour in enough water to cover almonds by 1-inch, stir in salt and then let soak for a minimum of 7 hours or 24 hours.

- Then drain the almonds and pat dry with paper towels.
- Switch on the dehydrator, then set it to 150 degrees F, and when it preheats, spread almonds in a single layer on the dehydrator trays with ½-inch space between the slices.
- Shut the dehydrator with its lid and then let the almonds dry for 12 to 24 hours until completely dry and pliable.
- When done, turn off the dehydrator, open the lid and let the almonds cool for 30 minutes at room temperature.
- Transfer the almonds into airtight containers, fill the containers about two-third, cover with the lids and store in a cool and dry place, away from heat or direct light.

Pecans

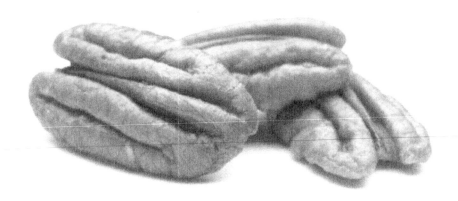

Preparation time: 10 minutes

Dehydration time: 24 hours

Ingredients:

- 4 cups pecans
- 1 tablespoon sea salt
- Water as needed

Instructions:

- Take a large bowl, add pecans, pour in enough water to cover almond by 1-inch, stir in salt and then let soak for a minimum of 7 hours or 24 hours.
- Then drain the pecans and pat dry with paper towels.
- Switch on the dehydrator, then set it to 150 degrees F, and when it preheats, spread pecans in a single layer on the dehydrator trays with ½-inch space between the slices.
- Shut the dehydrator with its lid and then let the pecans dry for 12 to 24 hours until completely dry and pliable.
- When done, turn off the dehydrator, open the lid and let the pecans cool for 30 minutes at room temperature.
- Transfer the pecans into airtight containers, fill the containers about two-third, cover with the lids and store in a cool and dry place, away from heat or direct light.

Pine Nuts

Preparation time: 10 minutes

Dehydration time: 24 hours

Ingredients:

- 4 cups pine nuts, skinless
- 1 tablespoon of sea salt
- Water as needed

Instructions:

- Take a large bowl, add pine nuts, pour in enough water to cover almond by 1-inch, stir in salt and then let soak for a minimum of 7 hours or 24 hours.
- Then drain the pine nuts and pat dry with paper towels.
- Switch on the dehydrator, then set it to 150 degrees F, and when it preheats, spread pine nuts in a single layer on the dehydrator trays with ½-inch space between the slices.
- Shut the dehydrator with its lid and then let the pine nuts dry for 12 to 24 hours until completely dry and pliable.

- When done, turn off the dehydrator, open the lid and let the pine nuts cool for 30 minutes at room temperature.
- Transfer the pine nuts into airtight containers, fill the containers about two-third, cover with the lids and store in a cool and dry place, away from heat or direct light.

Cashews

Preparation time: 10 minutes

Dehydration time: 24 hours

Ingredients:

- 4 cups cashews
- 1 tablespoon of sea salt
- Water as needed

Instructions:

- Take a large bowl, add cashews, pour in enough water to cover almond by 1-inch, stir in salt and then let soak for a minimum of 7 hours or 24 hours.

- Then drain the cashews and pat dry with paper towels.

- Switch on the dehydrator, then set it to 150 degrees F, and when it preheats, spread cashews in a single layer on the dehydrator trays with ½-inch space between the slices.

- Shut the dehydrator with its lid and then let the cashews dry for 12 to 24 hours until completely dry and pliable.

- When done, turn off the dehydrator, open the lid and let the cashews cool for 30 minutes at room temperature.

- Transfer the cashews into airtight containers, fill the containers about two-third, cover with the lids and store in a cool and dry place, away from heat or direct light.

Whole Grains

Preparation time: 5 minutes

Dehydration time: 6 hours

Ingredients:

- Rice or wheat, barley, oats, quinoa, corn, rye, spelt

Instructions:

- Place the grains into a colander and then rinse well under warm water until clean.
- Take a large pot half full with water, place it over high heat, stir in salt and then bring it to a boil.

- Add grains, stir, switch heat to medium-low level and then simmer for 15 to 30 minutes or more until cooked.
- When done, drain the grains and let them cool for 30 to 45 minutes until cooled.
- Switch on the dehydrator, then set it to 130 degrees F, line its tray with parchment paper, and when it preheats, spread grains in a single and thin layer.
- Shut the dehydrator with its lid, and then let the grains dry for 6 hours until completely dry and brittle.
- When done, turn off the dehydrator, open the lid and let the grains cool for 30 minutes at room temperature.
- Transfer the grains into plastic bags or airtight containers, fill the containers about two-third, cover with the lids and store in a cool and dry place, away from heat or direct light.

Legumes and Beans

Preparation time: 5 minutes

Dehydration time: 6 hours

Ingredients:

- Lentils, pulses, peas or beans

Instructions:

- Place legumes in a large bowl, cover with water by 1-inch, and let soak for a minimum of 6 hours or overnight.
- Then drain the legumes, transfer into a large bowl, and pour in enough cold water until covered.
- Place the pot over medium-high heat, bring it to a boil, then switch heat to the low level and simmer between 45 minutes to 2 hours and 30 minutes until softened.
- When done, remove the pot from heat, season legumes with salt, and let sit for 15 minutes, covering the pot with a lid.
- After 15 minutes, drain the legumes and set aside for 30 minutes until cooled.
- Switch on the dehydrator, then set it to 130 degrees F, line its tray with parchment paper, and when it preheats, spread legumes in a single and thin layer.
- Shut the dehydrator with its lid and then let the grains dry for 4 to 6 hours until completely dry and brittle.
- When done, turn off the dehydrator, open the lid and let the legumes cool for 30 minutes at room temperature.
- Transfer the legumes into plastic bags or airtight containers, fill the containers about two-third, cover with the lids and store in a cool and dry place, away from heat or direct light.

Pasta

Preparation time: 5 minutes

Dehydration time: 4 hours

Ingredients:

- Pasta, uncooked
- 1 tablespoon salt

Instructions:

- Place the pot over medium-high heat, stir in salt, and then bring it to a boil.
- Add pasta, cook for 10 to 15 minutes until tender, then drain into the colander and rinse immediately under cold water.
- Switch on the dehydrator, then set it to 135 degrees F, line its tray with parchment paper, and when it preheats, spread pasta in a single and thin layer.
- Shut the dehydrator with its lid, and then let the grains dry for 2 to 4 hours until completely dry and hard.

- When done, turn off the dehydrator, open the lid and let the pasta cool for 30 minutes at room temperature.
- Transfer the pasta into plastic bags or airtight containers, fill the containers about two-third, cover with the lids and store in a cool and dry place, away from heat or direct light.

Onion Soup Mix

Preparation time: 5 minutes

Dehydration time: 12 hours

Ingredients:

- ¼ cup onion flakes, dehydrated
- 1 teaspoon salt
- 1 teaspoon garlic powder
- ¼ teaspoon ground black pepper
- 1 teaspoon dried thyme
- 1 teaspoon mustard powder
- 1 teaspoon paprika

Instructions:

- Dehydrate onions by using the recipe of onion flakes from the vegetable section and then crumble onions into flakes.
- Take a small bowl, add onion flakes and remaining ingredients and then stir until mixed.
- Transfer the mix into a plastic bag or an airtight container, cover it with the lid, and then store it in a cool and dry place, away from heat or direct light.
- When ready to eat, place ½ cup of the mix in a large mug or bowl, pour in 1 cup of boiling water, stir until smooth and then serve.

Potato Soup Mix

Preparation time: 5 minutes

Dehydration time: 6 hours

Ingredients:

- 1 pound white potatoes
- 1¾ cup mashed potato flakes
- ¼ cup hash browns, dehydrated, crushed
- 2 tablespoons chicken bouillon granules
- ¼ teaspoon ground black pepper
- 2 teaspoons onion flakes
- 1 teaspoon seasoning salt
- ¼ teaspoon dried thyme
- ⅛ teaspoon turmeric powder
- 1½ cups of milk powder

Instructions:

- Dehydrate the hash browns, and for this, boil the white potatoes with their skin for 15 minutes or more until fully cooked and not too soft.
- When done, rinse potatoes under cold water, pat dry, peel the skins and grate potatoes.
- Switch on the dehydrator, then set it to 135 degrees F, line its tray with parchment paper and when it preheats, spread grated potatoes in a single and thin layer.
- Shut the dehydrator with its lid, and then let the grains dry for 6 hours until completely dry.
- When done, turn off the dehydrator, open the lid and let the grated potatoes cool for 30 minutes at room temperature.
- Dehydrate onions by using the recipe of onion flakes from the vegetable section and then crumble onions into flakes.
- Take a small bowl, add onion flakes, ¼ cup of dehydrated hash browns along with the remaining ingredients and then stir until mixed.

- Transfer the mix into a plastic bag or an airtight container, cover it with the lid, and then store it in a cool and dry place, away from heat or direct light.
- When ready to eat, place ½ cup of the mix in a large mug or bowl, pour in 1 cup of boiling water, stir until smooth and then serve.

Black Bean Soup Mix

Preparation time: 5 minutes

Dehydration time: 6 hours

Ingredients:

- 2 cans of black beans
- 2 tablespoons lime juice
- 1 can of diced tomatoes and green chili
- 1 teaspoon dried red peppers

- 1 teaspoon onion powder
- 1 teaspoon cilantro flakes
- 1 teaspoon garlic powder
- 1 ½ teaspoon salt
- 1 teaspoon ground white pepper
- 1 teaspoon red chili powder
- 2 teaspoons ground cumin

Instructions:

- Place all the ingredients in a food processor and then blend at high speed until smooth.
- Switch on the dehydrator, then set it to 145 degrees F, line its tray with parchment paper and when it preheats, spread black bean mixture in a single and thin layer.
- Shut the dehydrator with its lid, and then let the mixture dry for 6 hours until completely dry.
- When done, turn off the dehydrator, open the lid and let the mixture cool for 15 minutes at room temperature.
- Then break the dehydrated mixture into chunks, transfer into a blender and then pulse for 1 to 2 minutes at high speed until the mixture resembles powder.
- Transfer the mix into a plastic bag or an airtight container, cover it with the lid, and then store it in a cool and dry place, away from heat or direct light.
- When ready to eat, place 3 tablespoons of the mix in a large mug or bowl, pour in 1 cup of boiling water, stir until smooth, garnish with sour cream and then serve.

Potato and Chive Soup Mix

Preparation time: 5 minutes

Dehydration time: 6 hours

Ingredients:

- 1/3 cup potato flakes
- 1 tablespoon dried scallion
- 1/8 teaspoon onion powder
- 1 ½ teaspoon corn starch
- 1/8 teaspoon garlic powder
- ¼ cup of milk powder
- 1/8 teaspoon salt
- 2 tablespoons powdered chicken bouillon
- 1/8 teaspoon ground black pepper
- 2 tablespoons grated Parmesan cheese

Instructions:

- Use the recipe of potato flakes, onion, and dried scallion from the vegetable section.
- Take a small bowl, all the ingredients for the soup mix, and then stir until mixed.
- Transfer the mix into a plastic bag or an airtight container, cover it with the lid, and then store it in a cool and dry place, away from heat or direct light.
- When ready to eat, place ½ cup of the mix in a large mug or bowl, pour in 1 cup of boiling water, stir until smooth, let it rest for 10 minutes and then serve.

Broccoli and Cheddar Soup Mix

Preparation time: 5 minutes

Dehydration time: 8 hours

Ingredients:

- ½ cup dried broccoli

- 1/8 teaspoon onion powder
- 2 tablespoons chicken bouillon powder
- 1/8 teaspoon garlic powder
- 1 tablespoon cornstarch
- 1/8 teaspoon ground black pepper
- ¼ cup of milk powder
- ¼ cup cheddar cheese powder

Instructions:

- Take broccoli florets, rinse well under running water until clean, pat dry by using paper towels, and then cut into slices, about ¼-inch thick.
- Switch on the dehydrator, then set it to 125 degrees F, line its trays with parchment paper, and when it preheats, spread broccoli slices in a single layer.
- Shut the dehydrator with its lid, and then let the broccoli dry for 8 hours until completely dry.
- When done, turn off the dehydrator, open the lid and let the broccoli slices cool for 30 minutes at room temperature.
- Use onion powder from the recipe of onion from the section of vegetables.
- Prepare the mix, and for this, take a medium bowl, place ½ cup dehydrated broccoli florets, add remaining ingredients and then stir until mixed.
- Transfer the mix into a plastic bag or an airtight container, cover it with the lid, and then store it in a cool and dry place, away from heat or direct light.
- When ready to eat, place the mix in a large mug or bowl, pour in 1 ¾ cup of boiling water, stir until smooth, let it rest for 10 minutes and then serve.

Pumpkin and Carrot Soup

Preparation time: 5 minutes

Dehydration time: 8 hours

Ingredients:

- 4 large carrots, peeled, sliced
- 1 shallot, peeled, roasted
- 1 lime, juiced
- 1 large bunch cilantro, destemmed, leaves chopped
- 1 teaspoon salt
- 1 tablespoon fish sauce
- 1 tablespoon chicken bouillon powder
- 1 teaspoon Sriracha sauce
- 1 cup pumpkin puree, cubed

- ½ cup chicken stock
- 1 can of coconut milk, unsweetened

Instructions:

- Take a large pot, place it over medium-high heat, add all the ingredients in it, except for lime juice and cilantro, and bring the mixture to a simmer.
- Ladle the mixture into a blender and then pulse for 1 to 2 minutes until smooth.
- Let the mixture cool in the blender for 20 minutes, add lime juice and cilantro and then pulse until smooth.
- Switch on the dehydrator, then set it to 145 degrees F, line its trays with parchment paper and when it preheats, spread the mixture in a single and thin layer.
- Shut the dehydrator with its lid and then let the mixture dry for 6 to 8 hours until completely dry and brittle.
- When done, turn off the dehydrator, open the lid and let the mixture cool for 15 minutes at room temperature.
- Then break the dehydrated mixture into chunks, transfer into a blender and then pulse for 1 to 2 minutes at high speed until the mixture resembles powder.
- Transfer the mix into a plastic bag or an airtight container, cover it with the lid, and then store it in a cool and dry place, away from heat or direct light.
- When ready to eat, place ½ cup of the mix in a large mug or bowl, pour in 1 cup of boiling water, stir until smooth, and then serve.

Mushroom and Couscous Soup Mix

Preparation time: 5 minutes

Dehydration time: 12 hours

Ingredients:

- 1 ½ teaspoon dried tomato pieces
- 1/3 cup dried mushrooms, chopped
- 1 ½ tablespoons dried scallions
- 2 teaspoons onion powder
- 1/8 teaspoon ground black pepper
- 1/8 teaspoon garlic powder
- 1/4 teaspoon salt
- 1/8 teaspoon dried thyme
- 1 tablespoon beef bouillon powder
- 2 tablespoons couscous

Instructions:

- Use the recipe of dried tomato, dried scallion and onion powder from the vegetable section, prepare dehydrated mushroom from the mushroom section, and dried thyme from the herb section.

- Take a medium bowl, place all the ingredients in it, and then stir until mixed.

- Transfer the mix into an airtight container, cover it with the lids and then store it in a cool and dry place, away from heat or direct light.

- When ready to eat, place 3 tablespoons of the mix in a large mug or bowl, pour in 1 cup of boiling water, stir until smooth, and then serve.

Citrus, Berry and Apple Tea

Preparation time: 5 minutes

Dehydration time: 2 hours

Serving: 30 cups

Ingredients:

- 1 ½ pound roses petals
- ¾ cup dried orange
- ¾ cup dried strawberry
- ¾ cup dried apple
- ¾ cup dried mint
- 1 cup white tea

Instructions:

- Dehydrate the apple and orange slice by using citrus slices recipe from the fruit section and dehydrate the berries by using strawberries recipes from the fruit section.
- Dehydrate the rose, and for this, rinse the rose petals thoroughly and then pat dry them by using paper towels.
- Switch on the dehydrator, then set it to 90 degrees F or the lowest temperature, and when it preheats, arrange rose petals in a single layer on the dehydrator trays with ½-inch space between the slices.
- Shut the dehydrator with its lid and then let the berries dry for 2 hours or more until completely dry and pliable.
- When done, turn off the dehydrator, open the lid and let the rose cool for 1 hour at room temperature.
- Reserve ½ cup dried rose for the recipe, store remaining rose petals into airtight containers, and then store in a cool and dry place, away from heat or direct light.
- Prepare the tea mix, and for this, break the dried fruit slices and rose petals into smaller pieces, place them in a bowl, add remaining ingredients and then stir until mixed.
- Transfer the mix into an airtight container, cover it with the lids and then store it in a cool and dry place, away from heat or direct light.
- When ready to drink, place 2 tablespoons of the mix in a mug, pour in 1 cup of boiling water, and stir until smooth.
- Taste the tea to adjust the taste, let it steep for 10 minutes, and then serve.

Apple, Strawberries, Hibiscus and Rose Tea

Preparation time: 5 minutes

Serving: 60 cups

Ingredients:

- 4 cups dried apples
- ½ pound rose hips
- 4 cups dried strawberries
- ½ pound hibiscus flowers

Instructions:

- Take a large bowl, place all of the ingredients in it and then stir until mixed.
- Transfer the mix into an airtight container, cover it with the lids and then store it in a cool and dry place, away from heat or direct light.
- When ready to drink, place 2 tablespoons of the mix in a mug, pour in 1 cup of boiling water, and stir until smooth.
- Taste the tea to adjust the taste, let it steep for 10 minutes, and then serve.

Ground Turkey Jerky

Preparation time: 10 minutes

Dehydration time: 6 hours

Serving: 1/3 pound jerky

Ingredients:

- 1 pound ground turkey, chilled
- 1 lemon, juiced, zested
- 2 tablespoons onion flakes
- ½ teaspoon minced garlic
- 1 tablespoon sugar
- 1 teaspoon salt

- 2 teaspoons sweet paprika
- 1 teaspoon ground black pepper
- 1/8 teaspoon ground cayenne pepper
- 1 tablespoon soy sauce
- 1 tablespoon Worcestershire sauce
- 1 tablespoon olive oil

Instructions:

- Take a large bowl, place all the ingredients in it except for turkey and then stir until combined.
- Let the mixture stand for 15 minutes, add turkey, stir until combined, and then let it marinate for 1 hour in the refrigerator.
- Then switch on the dehydrator, then set it to 155 degrees F, and let it preheat.
- Meanwhile, take a large piece of parchment sheet, place one-fourth of the turkey mixture, cover with another piece of parchment sheet and then roll it to ¼-inch thickness.
- When dehydrator has preheated, remove the top sheet from turkey, place dehydrator tray on top, and then flip to transfer turkey mixture onto the tray.
- Remove the parchment sheet, poke some holes into the turkey by using a fork, shut the dehydrator with its lid, and then let the turkey dry for 4 to 6 hours until completely dry but not crunchy.
- When done, turn off the dehydrator, open the lid and let the jerky cool for 15 minutes at room temperature.
- Break dehydrated jerky into the piece and dehydrate the remaining turkey mixture in the same manner.
- Transfer jerky pieces into plastic bags, and then store them in a cool and dry place, away from heat or direct light.

Teriyaki Beef Jerky

Preparation time: 10 minutes

Dehydration time: 8 hours

Serving: 1/2 pound jerky

Ingredients:

- 1 pound London broil, 1/4-inch thick sliced
- 1 teaspoon onion powder
- ½ teaspoon garlic powder
- 1 tablespoon brown sugar
- 1/4 teaspoon ground black pepper
- 1 ½ teaspoons salt
- 1 tablespoon honey
- 2/3 cup teriyaki marinade

- 1 teaspoon soy sauce
- 1 teaspoon liquid smoke
- 1/4 cup water
- ½ cup orange juice

Instructions:

- Take a large bowl, place all the ingredients in it except for London broil and then whisk until the salt has dissolved.
- Pour the mixture into a large plastic bags, add beef slices, seal completely, shake to coat beef with the marinade and then let it marinate for a minimum of 24 hours in the refrigerator.
- Then switch on the dehydrator, then set it to 155 degrees F, and let it preheat.
- Meanwhile, remove beef slices from the marinade and then pat dry with paper towels.
- Spread beef slices on the dehydrator trays with the ½-inch distance between the slices, shut the dehydrator with its lid, and then let the beef dry for 4 to 8 hours until completely dry but not crunchy.
- When done, turn off the dehydrator, open the lid and let the jerky cool for 15 minutes at room temperature.
- Transfer jerky pieces into plastic bags and then store them in a cool and dry place, away from heat or direct light.

Chicken

Preparation time: 10 minutes

Dehydration time: 8 hours

Serving: 1

Ingredients:

- Large chicken, skinned, fat trimmed

Instructions:

- Prepare the chicken, and for this, rinse it thoroughly and then cut it in half.
- Take a large pot, place chicken pieces in it, cover with water, and then place the pot over medium-high heat.
- Cook the chicken for 1 hour or more until chicken starts falling apart, then transfer chicken to a cutting board and let it cool for 15 minutes.
- Separate the chicken meat from its bones by using two forks and then set aside until required.

- Switch on the dehydrator, then set it to 155 degrees F, and when it preheats, arrange chicken pieces in a single layer on the dehydrator trays with ½-inch space between the slices.

- Shut the dehydrator with its lid and then let the berries dry for 6 to 8 hours until completely dry.

- When done, turn off the dehydrator, open the lid and let the chicken cool for 30 minutes at room temperature.

- Check the dryness of chicken by breaking its slice in half, and there shouldn't be any moisture along the surface of the break.

- Transfer the chicken into a large plastic bag and then store it in a cool and dry place, away from heat or direct light.

Lamb Jerky

Preparation time: 10 minutes

Dehydration time: 6 hours

Serving: 1/2 pound jerky

Ingredients:

- 2 pounds leg of lamb, boneless, fat trimmed
- 1 teaspoon garlic powder
- 1 ½ teaspoons onion powder
- ½ teaspoon ground black pepper
- 1 tablespoon oregano
- 3 tablespoons Worcestershire sauce
- 1/3 cup soy sauce

Instructions:

- Place leg of lamb in a large plastic bag and let it freeze for 1 hour.
- Then prepare the marinade, and for this, take a small bowl, place remaining ingredients in it, and then whisk until combined.
- Remove lamb from the freezer, and then cut it into slices, about ¼-inch thick.
- Brush the lamb generously with the marinade, layer the slices in a 9-by-13 inches dish, cover the dish with plastic wrap, and then let it marinate for a minimum of 8 hours in the refrigerator.
- Then switch on the dehydrator, then set it to 145 degrees F, when it preheats, spread lamb slices on the dehydrator trays with the ½-inch distance between the slices.
- Shut the dehydrator with its lid, and then let the lamb slices dry for 6 hours until completely dry and crispy.

- When done, turn off the dehydrator, open the lid and let the jerky cool for 15 minutes at room temperature.
- Transfer jerky pieces into plastic bags, and then store them in a cool and dry place, away from heat or direct light.

Ground Beef

Preparation time: 10 minutes

Dehydration time: 6 hours

Serving: 1/2 pound

Ingredients:

- 1 pound ground beef or turkey
- ½ cup ground bread crumbs

Instructions:

- Take a large bowl, place ground beef in it, crumble it, then add bread crumbs and then stir until combined.

- Take a large frying pan, place it over medium-high heat, and when hot, add beef mixture and then cook for 10 to 15 minutes until cooked and light brown.
- When done, spread ground beef on a baking sheet lined with parchment sheet and let it rest for 10 minutes to remove excess moisture.
- Then switch on the dehydrator, then set it to 145 degrees F, and when it preheats, and spread ground beef in a single layer on the dehydrator trays lined with parchment paper.
- Shut the dehydrator with its lid, and then let the ground beef dry for 6 hours until completely dry.
- When done, turn off the dehydrator, open the lid and let the berries cool for 30 minutes at room temperature.
- Transfer the ground beef into plastic bags, and then store in a cool and dry place, away from heat or direct light.

Teriyaki Mushroom Jerky

Preparation time: 10 minutes

Dehydration time: 20 hours

Ingredients:

- 8 ounces portabella mushroom caps, about 2
  For the Marinade:
- 1 teaspoon grated ginger
- ½ teaspoon minced garlic
- 2 tablespoons brown sugar
- ¼ cup soy sauce
- 1½ teaspoon sesame oil
- 3 tablespoons rice vinegar
- 1 teaspoon Sriracha sauce

Instructions:

- Prepare the teriyaki sauce, and for this, take a large bowl, place all the ingredients for the marinade in it and then whisk until combined.
- Cut the mushrooms into 1/3-inch pieces, add to the marinade, toss until coated and then let marinate for a minimum of 8 hours at room temperature, tossing occasionally.
- Then switch on the dehydrator, then set it to 125 degrees F, and when it preheats, arrange mushroom slices in a single layer on the dehydrator trays with ½-inch space between the slices.
- Shut the dehydrator with its lid, and then let the mushrooms dry for 12 hours until completely dry but pliable.
- When done, turn off the dehydrator, open the lid and let the mushrooms cool for 30 minutes at room temperature.

- Serve straight away or transfer the mushrooms into airtight containers or a plastic bag, fill it about two-third, and then store in a cool and dry place, away from heat or direct light.

Salmon Jerky

Preparation time: 10 minutes

Dehydration time: 8 hours

Serving: 1/2 pound jerky

Ingredients:

- Salmon fillets, skinless
- 1 cup salt
- ¼ cup soy sauce
- 2 ½ cups brown sugar
- 1 gallon water

Instructions:

- Prepare the brine, and for this, take a large pot and add salt, sugar, water, and soy sauce.
- Place the pot over medium-high heat, boil until sugar has dissolved completely, remove the pot from the heat and then bring it to room temperature.
- Then cut the salmon into ¼-inch thick slices, add to the cooled brine and let them soak for 10 hours in the refrigerator, covering the pot with a lid.
- Then remove salmon slices from the brine, rinse well under running water and pat dry with paper towels.
- Switch on the dehydrator, then set it to 145 degrees F, when it preheats, spread salmon slices on the greased dehydrator trays with the ½-inch distance between the slices.
- Shut the dehydrator with its lid and then let the salmon slices dry for 6 to 8 hours until completely dry.
- When done, turn off the dehydrator, open the lid and let the jerky cool for 15 minutes at room temperature.
- Transfer jerky pieces into plastic bags, and then store in a cool and dry place, away from heat or direct light.

Tuna

Preparation time: 5 minutes

Dehydration time: 6 hours

Ingredients:

- Tuna, packed in water

Instructions:

- Drain the tuna and then break it into small pieces.
- Switch on the dehydrator, then set it to 145 degrees F, and when it preheats, arrange tuna pieces in a single layer on the dehydrator trays with ½-inch space between the slices.
- Shut the dehydrator with its lid, and then let the tuna dry for 6 hours until completely dry.
- When done, turn off the dehydrator, open the lid and let the tuna cool for 30 minutes at room temperature.
- Transfer tuna into a plastic bag, and then store it in a cool and dry place, away from heat or direct light.

Shrimps

Preparation time: 5 minutes

Dehydration time: 6 hours

Ingredients:

- Medium shrimps, frozen, peeled, deveined, precooked

Instructions:

- Thaw the frozen shrimps, and rinse them under ice-cold water.
- Pinch off the tails of shrimps, rinse and then slice each shrimp into five pieces.
- Switch on the dehydrator, then set it to 145 degrees F, and when it preheats, arrange shrimp pieces in a single layer on the dehydrator trays with ½-inch space between the slices.
- Shut the dehydrator with its lid and then let the berries dry for 6 hours until completely dry.

- When done, turn off the dehydrator, open the lid and let the shrimps cool for 30 minutes at room temperature.
- Transfer shrimps into a plastic bag, and then store in a cool and dry place, away from heat or direct light.

Crab

Preparation time: 5 minutes

Dehydration time: 6 hours

Ingredients:

- Imitation crab meat, refrigerated

Instructions:

- Prepare the crab meat, and for this, pull the meat into smaller pieces.

- Switch on the dehydrator, then set it to 145 degrees F, and when it preheats, arrange crab meat in a single layer on the dehydrator trays.
- Shut the dehydrator with its lid and then let the crab meat dry for 6 hours until completely dry.
- When done, turn off the dehydrator, open the lid and let the crab cool for 30 minutes at room temperature.
- Transfer shrimps into a plastic bag, and then store in a cool and dry place, away from heat or direct light.

Milk Powder

Preparation time: 5 minutes

Dehydration time: 12 hours

Ingredients:

- Skim milk, buttermilk, or almond milk

Instructions:

- Switch on the dehydrator, then set it to 135 degrees F, and then let it preheat.
- Meanwhile, line each dehydrator tray with a fruit roll insert and then pour 1 cup of the milk into each tray.

- Place the dehydrator trays in the preheated dehydrator, shut with its lid, and then let the milk dry for 12 hours or more until completely dry and flaky.
- When done, turn off the dehydrator, open the lid, let the milk cool for 30 minutes at room temperature, and then crumble it.
- Transfer milk crumbles into a blender and then pulse at high speed until powdered.
- Strain the milk powder into airtight containers or plastic bags and then store in a cool and dry place, away from heat or direct light.

Butter Powder

Preparation time: 5 minutes

Dehydration time: 10 hours

Ingredients:

- Butter, unsalted or butter substitute like nut butter, almond butter, peanut butter

Instructions:

- Place the butter in the freezer for 1 hour or more until solid enough to slice and then cut it into strips, ½-inch thick.
- Take a baking sheet, line it with parchment paper, spread butter slices on it, and let it freeze for 24 hours until solid.
- Switch on the dehydrator, then set it to 125 degrees F, and when it preheats, arrange butter slices in a single layer on the dehydrator trays lined with parchment paper with ½-inch space between the slices.
- Shut the dehydrator with its lid, and then let the butter dry for 8 to 10 hours until completely dry.
- When done, turn off the dehydrator, open the lid and let the butter cool for 10 minutes at room temperature.
- Place butter into a blender, pulse at high speed until powdered, transfer it into airtight containers and then store the butter powder in a cool and dry place, away from heat or direct light.

Eggs

Preparation time: 5 minutes

Dehydration time: 10 hours

Ingredients:

- 5 eggs, organic, at room temperature

Instructions:

- Switch on the dehydrator, then set it to 140 degrees F, and let it preheat.
- Meanwhile, take a large bowl, crack the eggs in it and then whisk until well blended and foamy.
- Take a fruit leather tray, and then pour blended eggs in it.
- Place the tray in the preheated dehydrator, shut the dehydrator with its lid, and then let the egg dry for 8 to 10 hours until completely dry and flaky.

- When done, turn off the dehydrator, open the lid and let the egg cool for 15 minutes at room temperature.
- Scrape the eggs, transfer into the plastic bag, seal it, and then let it freeze for a minimum of 1 hour.
- Then transfer egg into a blender, pulse at high speed until powdered, strain eggs evenly into five airtight containers or plastic bags, and then store in a cool and dry place, away from heat or direct light.
- When ready to use, add 1 tablespoon and 1 teaspoon cold water into each powdered egg and let it sit for 5 minutes or more until egg mixture resembles the state before it was dehydrated; add more water if needed.

Cheese

Preparation time: 5 minutes

Dehydration time: 12 hours

Ingredients:

- 1 piece of parmesan cheese, cheddar cheese, mozzarella cheese or cottage cheese

Instructions:

- Grate the cheese
- Switch on the dehydrator, then set it to 125 degrees F, and let it preheat.
- Meanwhile, grate the cheese by using a grater or vegetable peeler.
- Then line the dehydrator tray with parchment paper, spread grated cheese in a single and even layer.
- Shut the dehydrator with its lid and then let the cheese dry for 8 to 12 hours until completely dry and easily crumbled.
- Transfer cheese into a plastic bag, seal it, and then let it freeze for a minimum of 10 minutes.
- Then transfer cheese into a blender, pulse at high speed until powdered, strain into air-tight containers or plastic bags, and then store in a cool and dry place, away from heat or direct light.

Yogurt

Preparation time: 5 minutes

Dehydration time: 8 hours

Ingredients:

- Yogurt, low-fat

Instructions:

- Switch on the dehydrator, then set it to 135 degrees F, and then let it preheat.
- Meanwhile, line the dehydrator tray with parchment paper and then spread yogurt in a thin layer, about 1/8-inch thick.
- Place the dehydrator tray into the preheated dehydrator, shut with its lid, and then let the yogurt dry for 6 to 8 hours until completely dry and brittle, rotating tray every 2 hours and flipping yogurt halfway.
- When done, turn off the dehydrator, open the lid and let the yogurt cool for 15 minutes at room temperature.
- Transfer yogurt into a blender, pulse at high speed until powdered, strain into air-tight containers or plastic bags,

and then store in a cool and dry place, away from heat or direct light.

Pumpkin and Chia Oats

Preparation time: 5 minutes

Serving: 1

Nutrition Information per Serving:

324 Cal; 14.8 g Fat; 3.2 g Saturated Fat; 33.8 g Carbohydrates; 3.2 g Fiber; 5.1 g Sugars; 16 g Protein

Ingredients:

- 3 tablespoons oats, quick-cooking
- 1 tablespoon chia seeds
- 2 tablespoons pumpkin powder
- ½ teaspoon pumpkin spice

- 1 teaspoon brown sugar
- 2 tablespoons coconut milk powder

Instructions:

- Take a medium bowl, place all the ingredients in it, and then stir until well combined.
- Transfer the oats mixture into a plastic bag, and store in a cool and dry place, away from heat or direct light.
- When ready to eat, transfer oat mixture into a large bowl, pour in ¾ cup of water, stir until mixed and let it sit for a minimum of 4 hours or overnight.
- Serve straight away.

Buckwheat Granola

Preparation time: 15 minutes

Dehydration time: 32 hours

Serving: 16

Nutrition Information per Serving:

187 Cal; 9 g Fat; 1 g Saturated Fat; 26 g Carbohydrates; 5 g Fiber; 8 g Sugars; 5 g Protein

Ingredients:

- 1 large apple, cored, cut into wedges
- 2 ½ cups buckwheat groats
- ½ cup almonds, sliced
- ¼ cup pumpkin seeds
- 1 cup Medjool dates, pitted
- ¼ cup flax seeds
- ¼ cup sunflower seeds
- ¾ cup dried cranberries or dried blueberries
- ¼ cup sesame seeds
- ½ cup walnuts
- ½ teaspoon of sea salt
- 1 tablespoon ground cinnamon
- Water, ad needed

Instructions:

- Take a large bowl, place buckwheat groats in it, pour in enough to cover by 1-inch, and then let soak for a minimum of 8 hours.
- Then drain the groats in a colander, rinse thoroughly and let them sit for 8 hours, rinse halfway through.
- Meanwhile, take a medium bowl, place flax seeds in it, pour in water and then let soak for a minimum of 8 hours; and when done, drain and set aside until required.

- Meanwhile, take a medium bowl, place almond slices in it, cover with water, and then let soak for a minimum of 8 hours; and when done, drain the almonds and set aside until required.
- Meanwhile, take a medium bowl, place walnuts slices in it, cover with water and then let soak for a minimum of 8 hours; and when done, drain the walnuts and set aside until required.
- Meanwhile, take a medium bowl, place pumpkin seeds in it, cover with water and then let soak for a minimum of 4 hours; and when done, drain the seeds, rinse thoroughly, and set aside until required.
- Meanwhile, take a medium bowl, place sunflower seeds in it, cover with water and then let soak for a minimum of 4 hours; and when done, drain the seeds, rinse thoroughly, and set aside until required.
- Meanwhile, take a medium bowl, place sesame seeds in it, cover with water and then let soak for a minimum of 4 hours; and when done, drain the seeds, rinse thoroughly, and set aside until required.
- Meanwhile, take a medium bowl, place pitted dates in it, cover with warm water and let soak for 15 minutes; when done, drain the dates and transfer them into a food processor.
- Add apple wedges, pour in ½ cup water, and then puree the mixture until the smooth paste comes together.
- Pour the apple-date mixture into a large bowl, add remaining ingredients and stir until well-combined mixture comes together.
- Switch on the dehydrator, then set it to 115 degrees F, and then let it preheat.

- Line the dehydrator tray with parchment paper, place 3 cups of the batter on it, spread it into a ¼-inch thick layer, and repeat with the remaining batter.
- Arrange the dehydrator trays into the preheated dehydrator, shut the dehydrator with its lid, and then let the mixture dry for 8 hours.
- After 8 hours, flip the granola mixture, remove the parchment sheet, switch the temperature to 105 degrees F and continue drying for 24 hours until completely dry.
- When done, turn off the dehydrator, open the lid and let the granola cool for 30 minutes at room temperature.
- Bread the granola into chunks, transfer into plastic bags or airtight containers, and store in a cool and dry place, away from heat or direct light.
- When ready to eat, serve granola with milk or yogurt and nuts.

Brown Rice Cereal

Preparation time: 10 minutes

Serving: 1

Nutrition Information per Serving:

402 Cal; 12.3 g Fat; 2 g Saturated Fat; 66.4 g Carbohydrates; 4 g Fiber; 25.5 g Sugars; 9.1 g Protein

Ingredients:

- ¼ cup dehydrated cooked rice, powdered
- 1 teaspoon ground flaxseed
- 2 tablespoons dried diced apples
- ¼ teaspoon ground cinnamon
- 1 tablespoon brown sugar
- 1 teaspoon clarified butter
- 2 tablespoons milk powder, full-cream

Instructions:

- Use the recipe of whole grains to prepare dehydrated rice and use the recipe of Rose, Citrus, Berry and Apple Tea to prepare to dehydrate apple slices.
- Take a medium bowl, place all the ingredients in it except for butter and then stir until combined.
- Transfer the rice mixture into a plastic bag, place butter in a separate bag, and store it in a cool and dry place, away from heat or direct light.
- When ready to eat, take rice mixture in a medium bowl, pour in ½ cup boiled water, stir well and let the mixture sit for 5 minutes.
- Then stir in the butter and serve.

Chia Seeds Porridge

Preparation time: 5 minutes

Serving: 1

Nutrition Information per Serving:

490 Cal; 41 g Fat; 7 g Saturated Fat; 29.6 g Carbohydrates; 14.4 g Fiber; 3.5 g Sugars; 9.6 g Protein

Ingredients:

- 2 tablespoons coconut flour
- 1 tablespoon chia seeds
- 2 tablespoons ground flaxseed
- 2 teaspoons Swerve sweetener
- 2 tablespoons pecans, chopped
- 2 tablespoons coconut milk powder
- 1 teaspoon clarified butter

Instructions:

- Take a medium bowl, place all the ingredients in it except for butter and pecans and then stir until combined.

- Transfer the chia seeds mixture into a plastic bag, place butter and pecans in a separate bag, and store in a cool and dry place, away from heat or direct light.

- When ready to eat, take a medium pot, place chia seeds mixture in it, and pour in ½ cup water.

- Place the pot over medium heat, bring it to a boil, then switch heat to the low level and cook the porridge for 4 minutes until thickened to the desired level.

- When done, remove the pot from heat, transfer porridge to a bowl and then stir in butter and pecans.

- Serve straight away.

Buckwheat Porridge

Preparation time: 10 minutes

Dehydration time: 8 hours

Serving: 4

Nutrition Information per Serving:

155 Cal; 1 g Fat; 0.2 g Saturated Fat; 33 g Carbohydrates; 4.5 g Fiber; 1.5 g Sugars; 5.7 g Protein

Ingredients:

- 1 cup buckwheat groats
- ½ cup almonds, sliced
- Water as needed
- 1 cup almond milk, unsweetened

Instructions:

- Take a large bowl, place the buckwheat groats in it, pour in enough water to cover them, and then let soak for a minimum of 1 hour or overnight.
- Then drain the buckwheat groats into a colander, rinse thoroughly and drain.
- Transfer groats into a blender, add remaining ingredients, and then pulse a high speed until smooth.
- Switch on the dehydrator, then set it to 130 degrees F and then let it preheat.
- Meanwhile, line the dehydrator tray with a parchment sheet and then spread groats mixture in an even layer, about 1/8-inch.
- Place the dehydrator tray into the preheated dehydrator, shut the dehydrator with its lid, and then let the porridge dry for 6 to 8 hours until completely dry and brittle.
- Scrape the porridge, transfer into a blender, and then pulse at high speed until powdered.

- Strain the porridge evenly into four airtight containers or plastic bags and then store in a cool and dry place, away from heat or direct light.
- When ready to use, pour ¼ cup of hot water into each bag, let it sit for 5 minutes or until rehydrate and then serve with fruit slices.

Sweet Potato Chips

Preparation time: 10 minutes

Dehydration time: 20 hours

Serving: 2

Nutrition Information per Serving:

158 Cal; 5 g Fat; 1 g Saturated Fat; 26 g Carbohydrates; 6 g Fiber; 7 g Sugars; 2 g Protein

Ingredients:

- 2 medium sweet potatoes, peeled, sliced
- ½ teaspoon of sea salt
- 2 teaspoons coconut oil, melted

Instructions:

- Switch on the dehydrator, then set it to 125 degrees F, let it preheat.
- Meanwhile, take a large bowl, place sweet potato slices in it, drizzle with oil, season with salt and then toss until well coated.
- Arrange sweet potatoes slices in a single layer on the dehydrator trays with ½-inch space between the slices, shut the dehydrator with its lid, and then dry for 12 to 20 hours until dehydrated and crisp.
- When done, turn off the dehydrator, open the lid and let the chips cool for 30 minutes at room temperature.
- Check the dryness of chips by breaking its slice in half, and there shouldn't be any moisture along the surface of the break.
- Transfer the chips into plastic bags and store them in a cool and dry place, away from heat or direct light.

Potato Chips

Preparation time: 10 minutes

Dehydration time: 18 hours

Serving: 2

Nutrition Information per Serving:

120 Cal; 2 g Fat; 0 g Saturated Fat; 23 g Carbohydrates; 2 g Fiber; 2 g Sugars; 1 g Protein

Ingredients:

- 1 pound white potatoes, peeled, sliced
- 1 teaspoon salt
- ¾ teaspoon red chili powder
- 2 lemons, juiced
- Cooking oil spray

Instructions:

- Switch on the dehydrator, then set it to 125 degrees F, let it preheat.
- Meanwhile, peel the potatoes, cut into thin slices and then dip into lemon slices.
- Arrange the potato slices on the dehydrator trays with ½-inch space between the slices, spray with oil and then sprinkle with salt and red chili powder.
- Place the dehydrator trays in the preheated dehydrator, shut with its lid, and then dry for 10 to 18 hours until completely dry and crisp.
- When done, turn off the dehydrator, open the lid and let the chips cool for 30 minutes at room temperature.
- Check the dryness of chips by breaking its slice in half, and there shouldn't be any moisture along the surface of the break.

- Transfer the chips into plastic bags and store them in a cool and dry place, away from heat or direct light.

Corn Chips

Preparation time: 10 minutes

Dehydration time: 10 hours

Serving: 1

Nutrition Information per Serving:

140 Cal; 6 g Fat; 1 g Saturated Fat; 19 g Carbohydrates; 2 g Fiber; 4 g Sugars; 2 g Protein

Ingredients:

- 2 cups sweet corn

Instructions:

- Switch on the dehydrator, then set it to 115 degrees F, and let it preheat.

- Meanwhile, place corn into a blender and then pulse at high speed until creamy.
- Line a dehydrator tray with parchment paper, and then spread corn mixture into a thin layer, about 1/8-inch thick.
- Place the dehydrator tray into the dehydrator, shut with its lid, and then let the corn dry for 4 hours.
- Then remove dehydrator tray, score triangles on top of the corn mixture and then continue drying for 4 to 6 hours until completely dry and crisp.
- When done, turn off the dehydrator, open the lid and let the chips cool for 30 minutes at room temperature.
- Transfer the chips into plastic bags and store them in a cool and dry place, away from heat or direct light.

Parmesan Tomato Chips

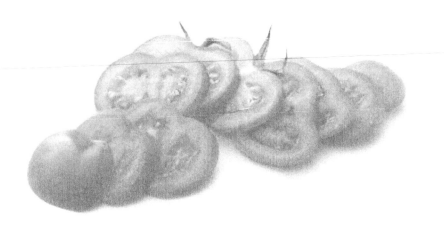

Preparation time: 10 minutes

Dehydration time: 24 hours

Serving: 3

Nutrition Information per Serving:

88 Cal; 5.8 g Fat; 1.1 g Saturated Fat; 9.4 g Carbohydrates; 2.1 g Fiber; 0.8 g Sugars; 2.5 g Protein

Ingredients:

- 3 cups sliced beefsteak tomatoes
- ½ teaspoon garlic powder
- 1 teaspoon of sea salt
- 1 tablespoon chopped parsley
- 1 tablespoon olive oil
- 1 tablespoon grated Parmesan cheese

Instructions:

- Take a medium bowl, place tomato slices in it, drizzle with oil and then toss until coated.
- Take a small bowl, place garlic powder in it and then stir in salt, parsley, and cheese until mixed.
- Take a dehydrator tray, arrange tomato slices in it with ½-inch space between the slices and then sprinkle with the garlic-cheese mixture.
- Switch on the dehydrator, then set it to 200 degrees F, and when it preheats, place the dehydrator tray in it, shut with its lid, and then let the tomato dry for 12 to 24 hours until completely dry and pliable.
- When done, turn off the dehydrator, open the lid and let the tomatoes cool for 30 minutes at room temperature.

- Check the dryness of tomatoes by breaking its slice in half, and there shouldn't be any moisture along the surface of the break.
- Transfer the tomatoes into plastic bags and store them in a cool and dry place, away from heat or direct light.

Fruit Roll-Ups

Preparation time: 10 minutes

Dehydration time: 11 hours

Serving: 2

Nutrition Information per Serving:

106.7 Cal; 0 g Fat; 0 g Saturated Fat; 26.7 g Carbohydrates; 4 g Fiber; 24 g Sugars; 0 g Protein

Ingredients:

- 2 cans of pineapple chunks, about 10 ounces or any fruit

Instructions:

- Drain the pineapples, transfer into a blender and then pulse at high speed until smooth.

- Switch on the dehydrator, then set it to 135 degrees F, and let it preheat.

- Meanwhile, take a dehydrator tray, line it with parchment paper, spread 1 ¼ cups of pineapple mixture on it in an even layer, about 1/8-inch, and then repeat with the remaining puree.

- Place the dehydrator tray in the preheated dehydrator, shut with its lid, and then let the pineapple dry for 9 to 11 hours until completely dry and pliable.

- When done, turn off the dehydrator, open the lid and let the pineapple leather cool for 30 minutes at room temperature.

- Break pineapple leather into pieces, roll each piece, then transfer the rolls into plastic bags, and store in a cool and dry place, away from heat or direct light.

Mixed Vegetables and Beans Soup

Preparation time: 5 minutes

Cooking time: 40 minutes

Serving: 4

Nutrition Information per Serving:

266.1 Cal; 1 g Fat; 0.2 g Saturated Fat; 52.6 g Carbohydrates; 14.7 g Fiber; 7.3 g Sugars; 14 g Protein

Ingredients:

- ½ cup dried pinto beans
- ¾ cup of corn bark
- ½ cup dehydrated small red beans

- ½ cup dehydrated mixed vegetables
- ½ cup dehydrated kidney beans
- 1/3 cup onion flakes
- ½ cup dried northern beans
- 1 tbsp dehydrated celery
- ½ cup dehydrated black-eye peas
- 2 bay leaves
- ¼ teaspoon salt
- 1/8 teaspoon ground white pepper
- ¼ teaspoon crushed red pepper
- 1/8 teaspoon ground black pepper
- ¼ teaspoon dried basil
- 2 cups chicken broth
- 2 cups water, at room temperature

Instructions:

- Use recipe of legumes and beans to dehydrate pinto beans, red beans, and kidney beans, use the recipe of frozen vegetables to dehydrate mixed vegetables, and then use the recipe of onion to make onion flakes.
- Take four plastic bags and evenly divide all the beans, peas, corn, and vegetables.
- Pack all the seasonings along with bay leaves separately among four small plastic bags and then store bean mixture and seasonings in a cool and dry place, away from heat or direct light.
- When ready to eat, take a medium pot, place beans mixture in it from one plastic bag, cover with warm water, and let soak for 15 minutes.

- Then place the pot over medium heat, pour in ½ cup chicken broth and water, stir in the seasonings, bring to a boil and continue boiling for 5 minutes.
- Switch heat to the low level, simmer the soup for 30 minutes, then remove the pot from heat and blend it until thickened slightly.
- Serve straight away.

Vegetable and Bean Soup with Garlic and Tomato

Preparation time: 5 minutes

Cooking time: 55 minutes

Serving: 4

Nutrition Information per Serving:

230 Cal; 7 g Fat; 2 g Saturated Fat; 30 g Carbohydrates; 10 g Fiber; 9 g Sugars; 11 g Protein

Ingredients:

- 14.5 ounces fire-roasted diced tomatoes with garlic
- 2 cups dried mixed vegetables
- ½ cup dried red beans
- 2 large red onions, peeled, diced
- ½ cup dried black beans
- 1 tablespoon minced garlic
- ½ teaspoon salt
- ¼ teaspoon ground black pepper
- 2 tablespoons vegetable powder
- ¼ teaspoon dried basil
- 1 tablespoon olive oil
- 9 cups of water

Instructions:

- Use recipe of legumes and beans to dehydrate beans, use the recipe of frozen vegetables to make dehydrated mixed vegetables, and make vegetable powder.
- Take a large plastic bag, transfer beans, and dried mixed vegetables in it, pack all the seasonings separately, and then store in a cool and dry place, away from heat or direct light.
- When ready to eat, take a large pot, place beans and vegetable mixture in it along with the seasonings, pour in water and let soak for 15 minutes.
- Then place the pot over medium-high heat, bring it to a boil, switch heat to medium level, and then simmer for 10 minutes.
- Meanwhile, take a medium skillet pan, place it over medium-low heat, add oil and when hot, add onions and garlic, and then cook for 5 minutes.

- Spoon the mixture into the pot, add tomatoes, switch heat to medium-high level, and then bring the mixture to a boil.
- Switch heat to medium-low level, simmer the soup for 45 minutes or more until thickened to the desired level, and then serve.

Eggplant Jerky

Preparation time: 10 minutes

Dehydration time: 18 hours

Serving: 2

Nutrition Information per Serving:

102 Cal; 7 g Fat; 3 g Saturated Fat; 6 g Carbohydrates; 0 g Fiber; 6 g Sugars; 2 g Protein

Ingredients:

- 2 large eggplants
- 1 tablespoon minced garlic
- 1 teaspoon of sea salt
- 2 teaspoons smoked paprika
- 1 teaspoon ground black pepper
- 1 cup balsamic vinegar
- 1 cup olive oil

Instructions:

- Prepare the eggplants, and for this, remove its stem and then cut it into jerky-sized slices, about ¼-inch thick.
- Prepare the sauce, and for this, take a large bowl, place all the remaining ingredients in it and then whisk until combined.
- Add eggplant pieces, toss until well coated with the sauce, and then let rest for a minimum of 2 hours at room temperature.
- Then switch on the dehydrator, then set it to 115 degrees F, and let it preheat.
- Meanwhile, line the dehydrator trays with parchment paper and then arrange eggplant slices in a single layer with ½-inch space between the slices.
- Place the dehydrator trays in the preheated dehydrator, shut with its lid, and then let the eggplant slices dry for 12 to 18 hours until completely dry but pliable.
- When done, turn off the dehydrator, open the lid and let the eggplant jerky cool for 30 minutes at room temperature.
- Serve straight away or transfer the eggplant jerky into airtight containers or a plastic bag, fill it about two-third, and then store in a cool and dry place, away from heat or direct light.

Buffalo Cauliflower Popcorn

Preparation time: 5 minutes

Dehydration time: 24 hours

Serving: 2 cups

Nutrition Information per Serving:

132 Cal; 10 g Fat; 6 g Saturated Fat; 26 g Carbohydrates; 2 g Fiber; 7 g Sugars; 4 g Protein

Ingredients:

- 2 medium heads of cauliflower, cut into small florets
  For the Buffalo Sauce
- ¼ cup sun-dried tomatoes
- ¾ cup Medjool dates, pitted
- 2 teaspoons onion powder

- 2 teaspoons garlic powder
- 1 teaspoon cayenne pepper
- ½ teaspoon turmeric powder
- 2 tablespoons nutritional yeast
- 2 tablespoons tahini
- ½ cup of water
- 1 tablespoon apple cider vinegar

Instructions:

- Prepare the sauce, and for this, place all of its ingredients in a blender and then pulse at high speed until smooth.
- Pour the sauce into a large bowl, add cauliflower florets and then toss until well coated.
- Then switch on the dehydrator, then set it to 115 degrees F, and let it preheat.
- Meanwhile, line the dehydrator trays with parchment paper and then arrange cauliflower florets in a single layer.
- Place the dehydrator trays in the preheated dehydrator, shut with its lid, and then let the cauliflower florets dry for 12 to 24 hours until completely dry and crispy.
- When done, turn off the dehydrator, open the lid and let the popcorns cool for 30 minutes at room temperature.
- Transfer the popcorns into plastic bags and store in a cool and dry place, away from heat or direct light.

Red Lentil Chili

Preparation time: 5 minutes

Cooking time: 30 minutes

Dehydration time: 10 hours

Serving: 4

Nutrition Information per Serving:

797 Cal; 24 g Fat; 10 g Saturated Fat; 122 g Carbohydrates; 30 g Fiber; 15 g Sugars; 36 g Protein

Ingredients:

- 1 cup red lentils, uncooked
- 14 ounces cooked kidney beans
- 2 cups sliced zucchini

- 14 ounces diced tomatoes, fire-roasted
- 1 cup diced green bell pepper
- 1 cup diced white onion
- 3 teaspoons minced garlic
- 1 teaspoon salt
- 3 tablespoons red chili powder
- 1 tablespoon ground cumin
- 1 teaspoon sugar
- 2 tablespoons tomato paste
- 1 tablespoon olive oil
- 2 cups vegetable broth

Instructions:

- Take a large pot, place it over medium heat, add oil and when hot, add onion and bell pepper, season with 1 teaspoon salt, and then cook for 7 to 10 minutes until softened.
- Add zucchini, cook for 10 minutes or until vegetables are softened, stir in garlic, red chili powder and cumin and then continue cooking for 30 seconds until fragrant.
- Add beans and tomatoes, stir in tomato paste, pour in the broth, stir until combined, and then bring it to a simmer.
- Add lentils, simmer the chili for 20 minutes until lentils have turned tender, and then stir in sugar; taste to adjust the seasoning.
- Remove the pot from the heat and let it cool for 10 minutes.
- Meanwhile, switch on the dehydrator, then set it to 135 degrees F, and let it preheat.
- Meanwhile, line the dehydrator trays with parchment paper and then spread chili in a thin layer on each tray.

- Place the dehydrator trays in the preheated dehydrator, shut with its lid, and then let the chili dry for 8 to 12 hours until completely dry and crumbly.
- When done, turn off the dehydrator, open the lid and let the chili cool for 30 minutes at room temperature.
- Break chili into small pieces, transfer evenly between four plastic bags, and store in a cool and dry place, away from heat or direct light.
- When ready to eat, place a medium pot over medium heat, add a bag of chili in it, pour in 1 cup water, stir in oil and then bring it to a boil.
- Then switch heat to medium level, cook the chili for 10 minutes until lentils and beans have turned tender and serve.

Vegetable Yellow Curry

Preparation time: 5 minutes

Cooking time: 10 minutes

Dehydration time: 8 hours

Serving: 2

Nutrition Information per Serving:

445 Cal; 17.2 g Fat; 5 g Saturated Fat; 61.1 g Carbohydrates; 6 g Fiber; 5.5 g Sugars; 7.6 g Protein

Ingredients:

- 1 ½ cup cooked white rice, cooled
- 2 cups frozen vegetable mix
- 1 tablespoon Thai yellow curry paste
- 4 tablespoons coconut milk powder

Instructions:

- Switch on the dehydrator, then set it to 135 degrees F, and let it preheat.
- Meanwhile, line the dehydrator trays with parchment paper and then spread rice, vegetables, and curry paste in a thin layer separately on each tray.
- Place the dehydrator trays in the preheated dehydrator, shut with its lid, and then let the chili dry for 4 to 8 hours until completely dry.
- When done, turn off the dehydrator, open the lid and let the rice, vegetables, and curry paste cool for 30 minutes at room temperature.
- Divide rice, vegetables, and curry paste evenly among four plastic bags, add coconut milk powder, and store in a cool and dry place, away from heat or direct light.

- When ready to eat, one packet of rice, vegetables and curry paste in a medium pot, place it over medium-high heat, pour in 2 cups water, and then bring the mixture to a boil.
- Then switch heat to medium-low heat, cook for 5 minutes, remove the pot from heat and let the mixture for 5 to 10 minutes until rehydrated.

Sriracha Chickpeas

Preparation time: 10 minutes

Dehydration time: 12 hours

Serving: 2

Nutrition Information per Serving:

110 Cal; 2 g Fat; 1 g Saturated Fat; 18 g Carbohydrates; 1 g Fiber; 4 g Sugars; 3 g Protein

Ingredients:

- 19-ounce cooked chickpeas
- 1 teaspoon salt
- 1 tablespoon sugar
- 3 tablespoons Sriracha sauce

Instructions:

- Take a large bowl, pour in Sriracha sauce, and then stir in salt.
- Pat dry chickpeas, add to the bowl, toss until coated with the sauce, and then sprinkle with sugar.
- Switch on the dehydrator, then set it to 130 degrees F, and let it preheat.
- Meanwhile, line the dehydrator trays with parchment paper and then spread chickpeas in a single layer.
- Place the dehydrator trays in the preheated dehydrator, shut with its lid, and then let the chili dry for 10 to 12 hours until completely dry.
- When done, turn off the dehydrator, open the lid and let the chickpeas cool for 30 minutes at room temperature.
- Transfer the chickpeas into airtight containers or plastic bags, and store in a cool and dry place, away from heat or direct light.

Chickpea and Spinach Curry

Preparation time: 5 minutes

Cooking time: 10 minutes

Serving: 1

Nutrition Information per Serving:

698 Cal; 33.2 g Fat; 10 g Saturated Fat; 85.7 g Carbohydrates; 6 g Fiber; 11.4 g Sugars; 19.9 g Protein

Ingredients:

- ¼ cup dehydrated white rice, cooked
- 1 tablespoon spinach powder
- ¼ cup dehydrated chickpeas
- ½ teaspoon salt
- ½ teaspoon curry powder
- 2 tablespoons coconut milk powder

Instructions:

- Use whole grain recipe to make dehydrated rice and chickpeas and use spinach recipe to create spinach powder.
- Take a large plastic bag, transfer curry mixture in it, and then store in a cool and dry place, away from heat or direct light.
- When ready to eat, place the curry mixture into a medium pot, place it over medium-high heat, and then pour in 1 cup water.
- Bring the mixture to a boil, cook for 10 minutes or until rehydrate and then remove the pot from heat.
- Serve straight away.

Lentil Stew

Preparation time: 5 minutes

Cooking time: 10 minutes

Dehydration time: 6 hours

Serving: 1

Nutrition Information per Serving:

286 Cal; 2.8 g Fat; 1 g Saturated Fat; 56.8 g Carbohydrates; 12 g Fiber; 4.4 g Sugars; 9.8 g Protein

Ingredients:

- ½ cup dehydrated white rice, cooked
- 2 tablespoons fried white onion
- ¼ cup dehydrated lentils
- ½ teaspoon salt
- ¼ teaspoon ground coriander
- ¼ teaspoon ground cumin
- 1 teaspoon chicken bouillon powder

Instructions:

- Use whole grain recipe to make dehydrated rice and use legumes recipe to create dehydrated lentils.
- Take a large plastic bag, transfer stew mixture in it, and then store in a cool and dry place, away from heat or direct light.
- When ready to eat, place the stew mixture into a medium pot, place it over medium-high heat, and then pour in 1 cup water.
- Bring the mixture to a boil, cook for 10 minutes or until rehydrate and then remove the pot from heat.
- Serve straight away.

Mushroom Risotto

Preparation time: 10 minutes

Cooking time: 15 hours

Serving: 1

Nutrition Information per Serving:

669 Cal; 7.2 g Fat; 2 g Saturated Fat; 117.3 g Carbohydrates; 12 g Fiber; 15 g Sugars; 25.7 g Protein

Ingredients:

- ½ cup dehydrated mushrooms
- ½ cup dehydrated Arborio rice, cooked
- ¼ teaspoon salt
- ½ teaspoon dried parsley

- ¼ teaspoon ground black pepper
- ¼ teaspoon dried thyme
- 2 tablespoons dehydrated grated parmesan cheese
- ¼ vegetable bouillon cube

Instructions:

- Use whole grain recipe to make dehydrated rice, use mushrooms recipe to create dehydrated mushroom, and use cheese recipe to make dehydrated parmesan cheese.
- Take a medium bowl, place rice and mushrooms in it, add salt, herbs, and bouillon cube and then stir until mixed.
- Take a large plastic bag, transfer rice-mushroom mixture in it, pack the cheese separately in other plastic bags, and then store in a cool and dry place, away from heat or direct light.
- When ready to eat, take a medium pot, add rice-mushroom mixture in it, pour in 1 cup of water, stir until mixed, and then let soak for 10 minutes.
- Then place the pot over medium heat, bring it to a boil, switch heat to the low level, and then cook for 10 to 15 minutes until dehydrated and rice have absorbed all the liquid.
- When done, remove the pot from heat and garnish the risotto with parmesan cheese.
- Serve straight away.

Beef Alfredo

Preparation time: 10 minutes

Cooking time: 15 hours

Serving: 1

Nutrition Information per Serving:

597 Cal; 27.4 g Fat; 2 g Saturated Fat; 51.4 g Carbohydrates; 6 g Fiber; 8.2 g Sugars; 34 g Protein

Ingredients:

- ½ cup dehydrated ground beef
- ¾ cup dehydrated pasta, cooked
- 1 teaspoon garlic powder
- ½ teaspoon salt
- 1 teaspoon all-purpose flour
- ¼ teaspoon ground black pepper
- 1 tablespoon milk powder, full-cream
- 2 tablespoons dehydrated cheddar cheese
- 1 tablespoon dehydrated mozzarella cheese

- 1 teaspoon clarified butter

Instructions:

- Use the ground beef recipe to make dehydrated beef, use the pasta recipe to create dehydrated pasta, and use cheese recipe to make dehydrated mozzarella and cheddar cheese.
- Prepare the beef Alfredo mixture, and for this, take a medium bowl, place beef and pasta in it, stir until mixed, and then transfer the mixture into a large plastic bag.
- Prepare the cheese sauce mixture, and for this, take a small bowl, place the remaining ingredients in it except for butter, stir until mixed, and packed it in a separate plastic bag.
- Store the beef Alfredo and the cheese sauce bags in a cool and dry place, away from heat or direct light.
- When ready to eat, take a medium pot, add beef alfredo mixture in it, pour in ¾ cup of water, stir until mixed, and then let soak for 5 minutes.
- Then place the pot over medium heat, bring it to a boil, switch heat to the low level, and then cook for 10 minutes until dehydrated.
- Remove pot from heat, add cheese sauce mixture, then stir in the ghee and serve.

Chickpea and Vegetable Curry

Preparation time: 10 minutes

Cooking time: 50 minutes

Dehydration time: 10 hours

Serving: 4

Nutrition Information per Serving:

499 Cal; 25 g Fat; 9 g Saturated Fat; 14.1 g Carbohydrates; 17.3 g Fiber; 19.1 g Sugars; 14.1 g Protein

Ingredients:

- 14 ounces cooked chickpeas
- 1 medium red onion, peeled, diced
- 3.3 pounds chopped mixed vegetables
- 2 teaspoons garam masala powder
- 1 teaspoon salt
- ½ teaspoon red chili powder
- 1 teaspoon turmeric powder

- 1 tablespoon coconut oil
- 8 tablespoons coconut milk powder
- ¼ cup chopped coriander

Instructions:

- Take a large saucepan, place it over medium heat, add oil and when hot, add onion and then cook for 5 minutes or until softened.
- Then add all the spices, stir until mixed, and cook for 1 minute until fragrant.
- Add mixed vegetables, pour in the water, stir until combined, then bring the mixture to a boil and adjust the seasoning to taste.
- Switch heat to medium-low level and then cook the vegetables for 30 minutes or more until tender, covering the pot with a lid.
- Add chickpeas, stir in coriander, cook for 2 minutes, then remove the pot from heat and let it cool for 10 minutes.
- Then switch on the dehydrator, then set it to 145 degrees F, and let it preheat.
- Meanwhile, line the dehydrator trays with a parchment sheet and then spread the curry in an even layer on each tray.
- Place the dehydrator trays into the preheated dehydrator, shut with its lid, and then let the curry dry for 8 to 10 hours until completely dry and brittle.
- When done, turn off the dehydrator, open the lid and let the curry cool for 30 minutes at room temperature.
- Scrape the curry, divide it evenly among four plastic bags and then store in a cool and dry place, away from heat or direct light.

- When ready to eat, place curry mixture from one packet into a medium pot, pour in 1 cup water, and place the pot over medium-high heat.
- Bring the curry to boil, then switch the heat to 10 minutes or until rehydrate and remove the pot from heat.
- Serve straight away.

Cheesy Salmon Pasta

Preparation time: 5 minutes

Cooking time: 10 minutes

Serving: 1

Nutrition Information per Serving:

517 Cal; 15.4 g Fat; 4 g Saturated Fat; 63.2 g Carbohydrates; 11 g Fiber; 1.9 g Sugars; 29.4 g Protein

Ingredients:

- 2/3 cup dehydrated pasta, cooked
- 2.5-ounces smoked salmon, dehydrate
- ½ teaspoon salt
- 1 teaspoon all-purpose flour
- 2 tablespoons powdered dehydrated cheddar cheese
- 1 tablespoon milk powder, full-cream
- 1 tablespoon clarified butter

Instructions:

- Use the pasta recipe to make dehydrated pasta, use the salmon recipe to make dehydrated salmon, and then use the cheese recipe to make powdered cheddar cheese.
- Prepare the cheese sauce mixture, and for this, take a small bowl, place cheese in it, add flour and milk powder, stir until mixed and transfer it in a plastic bag.
- Transfer and seal remaining ingredients separately in plastic bags and then store them in a cool and dry place, away from heat or direct light.
- When ready to eat, take a medium pot, add the pasta in it, pour in 1/3 cup of water, place the pot over medium heat, and then bring it to a boil.
- Switch heat to medium-low level, stir in salt and then cook the pasta for 5 minutes until rehydrated.
- Remove the pot from heat, add cheese sauce and milk, stir until mixed and then stir in butter until melts.
- Top pasta with salmon and then serve.

Mac and Cheese

Preparation time: 5 minutes

Cooking time: 10 minutes

Serving: 1

Nutrition Information per Serving:

445 Cal; 20.6 g Fat; 6 g Saturated Fat; 48.4 g Carbohydrates; 11 g Fiber; 5.6 g Sugars; 16 g Protein

Ingredients:

- 2/3 cup pre-cooked and dehydrated pasta
- ¼ teaspoon salt
- 1 teaspoon all-purpose flour
- 3 tablespoons powdered dehydrated Cheddar cheese
- 1 tablespoon milk powder, full-cream
- 1 tablespoon clarified butter

Instructions:

- Use the pasta recipe to make dehydrated pasta, and then use the cheese recipe to make powdered cheddar cheese.
- Prepare the cheese sauce powder, and for this, take a medium bowl, add flour in it, stir in cheese and milk powder, stir until mixed, and then transfer the mixture in a plastic bag.
- Transfer and store the remaining ingredients separately in plastic bags and then store them along with cheese sauce powder in a cool and dry place, away from heat or direct light.
- When ready to eat, take a medium pot, add the pasta in it, pour in 1/3 cup of water, place the pot over medium heat, and then bring it to a boil.
- Switch heat to medium-low level, stir in salt and then cook the pasta for 5 minutes until rehydrated.
- Remove the pot from heat, add cheese sauce and milk, stir until mixed and then stir in butter until melts.
- Serve immediately.

Ground Beef and Beans Chili

Preparation time: 10 minutes

Dehydration time: 10 hours

Serving: 3

Nutrition Information per Serving:

342.3 Cal; 19.1 g Fat; 7.7 g Saturated Fat; 25.5 g Carbohydrates; 5 g Fiber; 7.6 g Sugars; 18.1 g Protein

Ingredients:

- 1 large white onion, peeled, chopped
- 1 pound ground beef
- 15 ounces cooked red beans
- ½ cup ground bread crumbs

- ½ teaspoon minced garlic
- 14 ounces diced tomatoes
- ¾ teaspoon salt
- 3 tablespoons red chili powder
- 10 ounces tomato puree

Instructions:

- Take a large bowl, place ground beef in it, add bread crumbs and then stir until combined, set aside until required.
- Take a medium pot, place it over medium heat, add oil and when hot, add onion and garlic, and cook for 5 minutes until softened.
- Add ground beef, cook it for 10 minutes or until browned, then stir in red chili powder and cook for 1 minute.
- Add beans, tomatoes, and tomato puree, stir until mixed and simmer the chili for 1 hour until cooked.
- When done, remove the pot from heat and let the chili cool for 10 minutes.
- Then switch on the dehydrator, then set it to 145 degrees F, and let it preheat.
- Meanwhile, line the dehydrator trays with parchment paper and then spread chili in a thin layer on each tray.
- Place the dehydrator trays in the preheated dehydrator, shut with its lid, and then let the chili dry for 8 to 10 hours until completely dry and crumbly.
- When done, turn off the dehydrator, open the lid and let the chili cool for 30 minutes at room temperature.
- Break chili into small pieces, transfer evenly between three plastic bags, and store in a cool and dry place, away from heat or direct light.

- When ready to eat, place a medium pot over medium heat, add a bag of chili in it, pour in 1 cup water, stir in oil and then bring it to a boil.
- Then switch heat to medium level, cook the chili for 1 minute or until rehydrate, and serve with pita chips.

Taco Stew

Preparation time: 10 minutes

Cooking time: 30 minutes

Dehydration time: 12 hours

Serving: 4

Nutrition Information per Serving:

532 Cal; 19.4 g Fat; 4 g Saturated Fat; 31 g Carbohydrates; 5.1 g Fiber; 8.3 g Sugars; 58.6 g Protein

Ingredients:

- 14 ounces cooked black beans
- 2.2 pounds ground turkey
- 1 medium red onion, peeled, chopped
- 12 ounces sweet corn
- 2 medium red bell pepper, cored, chopped
- 14 ounces diced tomatoes
- 1 bunch of cilantro, destemmed, leaves chopped
- 1 teaspoon salt
- 2 teaspoons taco spice mixture
- 1 tablespoon olive oil
- 1 tablespoon powdered dehydrated cheddar cheese
- Corn chips, crumbled, for serving

Instructions:

- Take a large saucepan, place it over medium heat, add oil and when hot, add onion and then cook for 5 minutes or until softened.
- Add ground turkey, stir until mixed, cook for 10 minutes until browned and then transfer meat mixture to a colander for draining it well.
- Then return turkey mixture into the saucepan, add beans, corn, and red pepper, stir in taco spice mix and continue cooking for 5 minutes.
- Add tomatoes along with their juice, stir until mixed, bring the mixture to a boil and then stir in cilantro.
- Season the mixture with salt, switch heat to the low level, and then cook for 15 minutes, covering the pan with a lid.
- After 15 minutes, remove the pan from heat and then let it cool completely.

- Then switch on the dehydrator, then set it to 145 degrees F, and let it preheat.
- Meanwhile, line the dehydrator trays with parchment paper and then spread stew in a thin layer on each tray.
- Place the dehydrator trays in the preheated dehydrator, shut with its lid, and then let the chili dry for 8 to 12 hours until completely dry and brittle.
- When done, turn off the dehydrator, open the lid and let the stew cool for 30 minutes at room temperature.
- Transfer the stew evenly among four plastic bags, pack cheese in separate plastic bags and then store in a cool and dry place, away from heat or direct light.
- When ready to eat, place stew from one plastic bag in a medium pot, pour in 1 cup water, place the pot over medium heat and then bring it to a boil.
- Bring the stew to a boil, cook it for 5 minutes, remove the pot from heat and then let the stew stand for 5 minutes or until rehydrated.
- Stir in the cheese, garnish with corn chips and then serve.

Jarred Garden Vegetable Soup

Preparation time: 10 minutes

Cooking time: 1 hour and 40 minutes

Serving: 5

Nutrition Information per Serving:

23 Cal; 0 g Fat; 0 g Saturated Fat; 5 g Carbohydrates; 1 g Fiber; 1 g Sugars; 1 g Protein

Ingredients:

- ¼ cup dehydrated sliced summer squash
- ¼ cup dehydrated shredded cabbage
- ½ cup dehydrated sliced potatoes
- ¼ cup dehydrated sliced zucchini
- 2 tablespoons dehydrated sliced onions
- ¼ cup dehydrated sliced carrots
- ¼ cup dehydrated sliced tomatoes
- ¼ cup dehydrated sliced green onions

- 2 tablespoons dehydrated vegetable stock

Instructions:

- Take a 1-quarts jar or five plastic bags, and then evenly layer with all the dehydrated sliced vegetables in it.
- Top with vegetable stock powder and then store in a cool and dry place, away from heat or direct light.
- When ready to eat, take a large pot, place soup mix in it, pour in 4 cups water, and then stir until mixed.
- Place the pot over medium heat, bring the soup to boil, then switch heat to the low level and simmer the soup for 1 hour and 30 minutes until vegetables have turned tender and soup reached to desired consistency.
- Ladle soup into bowls and then serve.

Flax Seed Bread

Preparation time: 10 minutes

Dehydration time: 24 hours

Serving: 12 slices

Nutrition Information per Serving:

192 Cal; 17 g Fat; 2 g Saturated Fat; 9 g Carbohydrates; 4 g Fiber; 12 g Sugars; 5 g Protein

Ingredients:

- 1 cup flax seeds
- 2 cups white onion quarters
- 1 ½ cups chopped tomato

- 1 tablespoon fresh rosemary
- 1 teaspoon of sea salt
- 1 tablespoon fresh thyme
- 1 cup sunflower seeds
- ¼ cup olive oil

Instructions:

- Place all the seeds in a food processor and then pulse for 30 seconds at high speed until grounded.
- Add remaining ingredients, pulse for 10 seconds until chunky batter comes together, and then spread the batter evenly on parchment-lined dehydrator trays, about 1/8-inch thickness.
- Switch on the dehydrator, then set it to 115 degrees F, and when it preheats, place dehydrator trays in it.
- Shut the dehydrator with its lid, let the bread dry for 12 hours, flip the bread, remove the parchment paper and continue dehydrating for another 12 hours until completely dry.
- When done, turn off the dehydrator, open the lid, let the bread cool for 30 minutes at room temperature, and then cut it into twelve slices.
- Transfer the bread slices into plastic bags and store them in a cool and dry place, away from heat or direct light.

Bread Crumbs

Preparation time: 5 minutes

Dehydration time: 4 hours

Serving: 8

Nutrition Information per Serving:

358 Cal; 7.4 g Fat; 0.8 g Saturated Fat; 61.7 g Carbohydrates; 61.7 g Fiber; 5.1 g Sugars; 9.2 g Protein

Ingredients:

- 1 bread, cut into eight slices or pita bread

Instructions:

- Switch on the dehydrator, then set it to 125 degrees F, and when it preheats, arrange bread slices in a single layer on the dehydrator trays with ½-inch space between the slices.
- Shut the dehydrator with its lid, and then let the bread dry for 3 to 4 hours until completely dry and crisp.
- When done, turn off the dehydrator, open the lid and let the bread cool for 15 minutes at room temperature.

- Transfer bread slices into a blender and then pulse at high speed until the mixture resembles fine crumbs.
- Transfer the bread crumbs into plastic bags, and store in a cool and dry place, away from heat or direct light.

Peanut Butter and Banana Graham Crackers

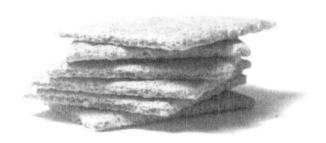

Preparation time: 15 minutes

Dehydration time: 4 hours

Serving: 50

Nutrition Information per Serving:

349.1 Cal; 19.9 g Fat; 3.4 g Saturated Fat; 36.5 g Carbohydrates; 4.5 g Fiber; 15.8 g Sugars; 11.1 g Protein

Ingredients:

- 2 ½ cups graham cracker crumbs
- 3 bananas, peeled, sliced

- ½ teaspoon cinnamon
- 1 cup ground peanuts
- ½ cup peanut butter, unsalted

Instructions:

- Take a large bowl, place bananas in it, mash them by using a fork and then stir in peanut butter until creamy mixture comes together.
- Add remaining ingredients, stir until well combined, and then shape the mixture into a dough ball.
- Place a large piece of waxed paper on clean working space, place the dough on it, and then shape it into a long rectangle by using a rolling pin.
- Wrap the dough with another waxed paper, let it chill in the refrigerator for a minimum of 4 hours, and then cut it into fifty ¼-inch thick slices.
- Switch on the dehydrator, then set it to 145 degrees F, and when it preheats, arrange crackers slices in a single layer on the dehydrator trays with ½-inch space between the slices.
- Shut the dehydrator with its lid and then let the crackers dry for 4 to 6 hours until completely dry and firm.
- When done, turn off the dehydrator, open the lid and let the crackers cool for 30 minutes at room temperature.
- Transfer the crackers into plastic bags and store them in a cool and dry place, away from heat or direct light.

Bagel Flax Crackers

Preparation time: 10 minutes

Dehydration time: 24 hours

Serving: 24

Nutrition Information per Serving:

44 Cal; 3 g Fat; 0 g Saturated Fat; 3 g Carbohydrates; 2 g Fiber; 0 g Sugars; 1 g Protein

Ingredients:

- ¾ cup golden flax seeds
- 3 teaspoons poppy seeds
- ¼ cup brown flax seeds
- 3 teaspoons sesame seeds
- 3 teaspoons onion flakes
- 3 teaspoons sea salt
- 3 teaspoons garlic powder
- ½ teaspoon minced garlic
- 1 1/2 cups water

Instructions:

- Pour water into a blender, add minced garlic and then pulse at high speed until blended.

- Pour the garlic water in a large bowl, add flax seeds and then let soak for 4 hours.

- Meanwhile, prepare spice mixture, and for this, place all the remaining ingredients in it except for salt, stir until mixed, and then set aside until required.

- After 4 hours, take a parchment-lined dehydrating tray, spread flax seeds mixture on them, about ¼-inch thick, and then score twenty-four squares on top.

- Sprinkle seasoning mix over cracker mixture, and sprinkle with salt.

- Switch on the dehydrator, then set it to 110 degrees F, and when it preheats, place dehydrator trays in it, shut with its lid, and then let the crackers dry for 24 hours until dry and crispy.

- When done, turn off the dehydrator, open the lid and let the crackers cool for 30 minutes at room temperature.

- Break crackers into pieces, then transfer them into plastic bags, and store in a cool and dry place, away from heat or direct light.

Caramel Apple Chips

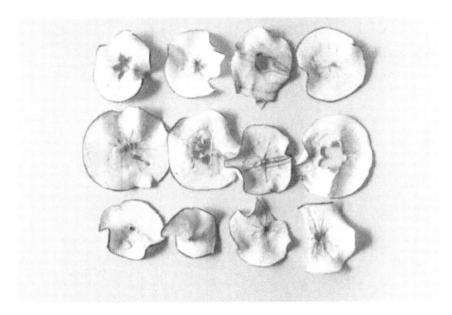

Preparation time: 5 minutes

Dehydration time: 14 hours

Serving: 4

Nutrition Information per Serving:

50 Cal; 0 g Fat; 0 g Saturated Fat; 12 g Carbohydrates; 3 g Fiber; 10 g Sugars; 0 g Protein

Ingredients:

- 4 medium green apples, cored, thinly sliced
- Caramel sauce as needed

Instructions:

- Prepare the chips, and for this, core the apples, cut them into thin slices, and then brush with caramel sauce on each side.
- Switch on the dehydrator, then set it to 110 degrees F, and when it preheats, arrange apple slices in a single layer on the dehydrator trays with ½-inch space between the slices.
- Shut the dehydrator with its lid, and then let the apple dry for 14 hours until completely dry and crispy.
- When done, turn off the dehydrator, open the lid and let the apple chips cool for 30 minutes at room temperature.
- Transfer the chips into plastic bags and store them in a cool and dry place, away from heat or direct light.

Apple and Flax Seeds Cookies

Preparation time: 10 minutes

Dehydration time: 6 hours

Serving: 30 cookies

Nutrition Information per Serving:

72 Cal; 1.8 g Fat; 0.2 g Saturated Fat; 12.3 g Carbohydrates; 2.2 g Fiber; 3.6 g Sugars; 2 g Protein

Ingredients:

- 2 medium apples, cored, chopped
- ½ cup Medjool dates, pitted
- 4 cup oats
- 4 tablespoons flax seeds
- ½ cup sliced almonds
- 1 teaspoon ground cinnamon

Instructions:

- Place all the ingredients in a blender except for oats and then pulse at high speed until the dough comes together.
- Transfer the dough into a bowl, add oats, stir until well combined, shape the mixture into thirty balls and then flatten each ball to make a ¼-inch cookie.
- Switch on the dehydrator, then set it to 113 degrees F, and when it preheats, arrange cookies in a single layer on the dehydrator trays with ½-inch space between the slices.
- Shut the dehydrator with its lid, let the cookies dry for 4 hours, then flip the cookies and dry for 2 hours until completely dry.
- When done, turn off the dehydrator, open the lid and let the cookies cool for 30 minutes at room temperature.
- Transfer the cookies into plastic bags and store them in a cool and dry place, away from heat or direct light.

Raisin Cookies

Preparation time: 10 minutes

Dehydration time: 24 hours

Serving: 20 cookies

Nutrition Information per Serving:

71.8 Cal; 2.5 g Fat; 0.4 g Saturated Fat; 11.3 g Carbohydrates; 1 g Fiber; 0 g Sugars; 1.5 g Protein

Ingredients:

- 3 medium apples, cored, chopped
- 1 cup soaked Medjool dates, pitted
- 3 medium bananas, peeled, sliced
- 1 tablespoon grated ginger
- ¾ cups ground sunflower seeds
- 1 cup raisins

- 1/8 teaspoon sea salt
- 2 tablespoons apple pie spice
- 1 tablespoon vanilla extract, unsweetened
- 2 tablespoons water

Instructions:

- Place all the ingredients in a blender except for raisins and then pulse at high speed until the dough comes together.
- Transfer the dough into a bowl, add raisins, stir until well combined, shape the mixture into twenty balls and then flatten each ball to make a ¼-inch cookie.
- Switch on the dehydrator, then set it to 104 degrees F, and when it preheats, arrange cookies in a single layer on the dehydrator trays with ½-inch space between the slices.
- Shut the dehydrator with its lid, and let the cookies dry for 18 to 24 hours until completely dry, flipping halfway through.
- When done, turn off the dehydrator, open the lid and let the cookies cool for 30 minutes at room temperature.
- Transfer the cookies into plastic bags and store them in a cool and dry place, away from heat or direct light.

Marshmallows

Preparation time: 5 minutes

Dehydration time: 3 hours

Serving: 4

Nutrition Information per Serving:

22 Cal; 0 g Fat; 0 g Saturated Fat; 6 g Carbohydrates; 0 g Fiber; 4.1 g Sugars; 0.1 g Protein

Ingredients:

- 1 bag of marshmallows

Instructions:

- Switch on the dehydrator, then set it to 160 degrees F, and when it preheats, arrange marshmallows in a single layer on the dehydrator trays with ½-inch space between the slices.
- Shut the dehydrator with its lid and then let the marshmallows dry for 2 to 3 hours until completely dry.

- When done, turn off the dehydrator, open the lid and let the marshmallows cool for 30 minutes at room temperature.
- Transfer the marshmallows into airtight glass containers or plastic bags, and store in a cool and dry place, away from heat or direct light.

Peanut Butter Balls

Preparation time: 10 minutes

Dehydration time: 12 hours

Serving: 2

Nutrition Information per Serving:

103.1 Cal; 4.3 g Fat; 0.7 g Saturated Fat; 15.4 g Carbohydrates; 0.8 g Fiber; 11.4 g Sugars; 2.3 g Protein

Ingredients:

- 2 cups dried apples, chopped

- 2 cups shredded coconut, unsweetened
- 1 ½ teaspoon vanilla extract, unsweetened
- 2/3 cup peanut butter, unsalted

Instructions:

- Take a large bowl, place all the ingredients in it, stir until well mixed and then shape the mixture into twenty balls.
- Switch on the dehydrator, then set it to 135 degrees F, and when it preheats, arrange balls in a single layer on the dehydrator trays with ½-inch space between the slices.
- Shut the dehydrator with its lid, and then let the balls dry for 10 to 12 hours until completely dry and crispy.
- When done, turn off the dehydrator, open the lid and let the balls cool for 30 minutes at room temperature.
- Transfer the balls into plastic bags and store them in a cool and dry place, away from heat or direct light.

Chocolate and Almond Smoothie

Preparation time: 5 minutes

Dehydration time: 12 hours

Serving: 1

Nutrition Information per Serving:

562 Cal; 44.4 g Fat; 12 g Saturated Fat; 7.2 g Carbohydrates; 8.3 g Fiber; 20.5 g Sugars; 7.2 g Protein

Ingredients:

- 3/4 cup almond milk, unsweetened
- 1 tablespoon peanut butter, unsalted
- 2 tablespoons rolled oats
- 1 medium banana, peeled
- 1 teaspoon ground flaxseed

- 1 teaspoon cocoa powder, unsweetened

Instructions:

- Place all the ingredients in a food processor and then pulse at high speed until smooth.
- Switch on the dehydrator, then set it to 115 degrees F, and when it preheats, spread smoothie mixture on parchment-lined dehydrating trays.
- Shut the dehydrator with its lid, and then let the smoothie dry for 6 to 12 hours until completely dry and brittle.
- When done, turn off the dehydrator, open the lid and let the berries cool for 30 minutes at room temperature.
- Transfer dried smoothie into a blender and then pulse at high speed until powdered.
- Transfer the smoothie powder into a plastic bag and store it in a cool and dry place, away from heat or direct light.
- When ready to drink, place smoothie powder into a large glass, pour in 2/3 cup of water, and then stir until well mixed.
- Let the smoothie stand for 5 minutes until rehydrate, stir again, and then serve.

Mango and Coconut Smoothie

Preparation time: 5 minutes

Dehydration time: 12 hours

Serving: 1

Nutrition Information per Serving:

578 Cal; 47 g Fat; 8 g Saturated Fat; 42.4 g Carbohydrates; 8.9 g Fiber; 27.7 g Sugars; 5.8 g Protein

Ingredients:

- 3/4 cup coconut milk, unsweetened
- 1 cup frozen mango chunks
- 2 tablespoons rolled oats
- 2 tablespoons shredded coconut, unsweetened

Instructions:

- Place all the ingredients in a food processor and then pulse at high speed until smooth.

- Switch on the dehydrator, then set it to 115 degrees F, and when it preheats, spread smoothie mixture on parchment-lined dehydrating trays.
- Shut the dehydrator with its lid, and then let the smoothie dry for 6 to 12 hours until completely dry and brittle.
- When done, turn off the dehydrator, open the lid and let the berries cool for 30 minutes at room temperature.
- Transfer dried smoothie into a blender and then pulse at high speed until powdered.
- Transfer the smoothie powder into a plastic bag, and store in a cool and dry place, away from heat or direct light.
- When ready to drink, place smoothie powder into a large glass, pour in 2/3 cup of water, and then stir until well mixed.
- Let the smoothie stand for 5 minutes or until rehydrated, stir again, and then serve.

Berry Smoothie

Preparation time: 5 minutes

Dehydration time: 6 hours

Serving: 1

Nutrition Information per Serving:

298 Cal; 2 g Fat; 0.3 g Saturated Fat; 68.1 g Carbohydrates; 9.4 g Fiber; 38.4 g Sugars; 4.8 g Protein

Ingredients:

- 2/3 cup orange juice
- 2 tablespoons rolled oats
- 1 medium banana, peeled
- 1 cup of frozen mixed berries

Instructions:

- Place all the ingredients in a food processor and then pulse at high speed until smooth.

- Switch on the dehydrator, then set it to 115 degrees F, and when it preheats, spread smoothie mixture on parchment-lined dehydrating trays.
- Shut the dehydrator with its lid, and then let the smoothie dry for 6 to 12 hours until completely dry and brittle.
- When done, turn off the dehydrator, open the lid and let the berries cool for 30 minutes at room temperature.
- Transfer dried smoothie into a blender and then pulse at high speed until powdered.
- Transfer the smoothie powder into a plastic bag and store it in a cool and dry place, away from heat or direct light.
- When ready to drink, place smoothie powder into a large glass, pour in 2/3 cup of water, and then stir until well mixed.
- Let the smoothie stand for 5 minutes until rehydrated, stir again, and then serve.

Conclusion

Dehydrating is a great way to do a variety of things that will serve you in the long run. It is a great way to preserve surplus amounts of food so that they remain in your possession for a big period. Many people might have a misconception that storing food may make them less appetizing, but by concentrating the flavors, it increases its tastiness.

In the time of emergencies, you don't know what might come in handy. One thing you will need is food supply. If you are going to a remote area where there are limited supplies and resources, dehydration can solve your problems. Hikers, campers, and even astronauts use this technique, so don't waste time and start dehydrating your food.

Most of us settle ourselves in our daily routine, not even thinking about doing something new due to fear. It's very healthy to engage in different activities, and there is no fear of dehydrating your food. It's perfectly safe, if not healthier, and can give you a range of flavor profiles you have never tasted before.

I hope that you enjoy dehydrating and eating your food.

Good luck on your dehydrating journey!

Printed in Great Britain
by Amazon